Biography Today

Profiles of People of Interest to Young Readers

Volume 13
Issue 3
September 2004

Cherie D. Abbey
Managing Editor

Kevin Hillstrom
Editor

Omnigraphics

615 Griswold Street
Detroit, Michigan 48226

Cherie D. Abbey, *Managing Editor*
Kevin Hillstrom, *Editor*

Peggy Daniels, Leif Gruenberg, Laurie Lanzen Harris, Jeff Hill,
Laurie Hillstrom, Sara Pendergast, Tom Pendergast, Diane Telgen,
Sue Ellen Thompson, Matt Totsky, and Rhoda Wilburn, *Sketch Writers*

Barry Puckett, *Research Associate*

Allison A. Beckett, Mary Butler, and Linda Strand, *Research Assistants*

Omnigraphics, Inc.

* * *

Matthew P. Barbour, *Senior Vice President*
Kay Gill, *Vice President — Directories*
Kevin Hayes, *Operations Manager*
Leif Gruenberg, *Development Manager*
David P. Bianco, *Marketing Manager*

* * *

Peter E. Ruffner, *Publisher*
Frederick G. Ruffner, Jr., *Chairman*

Copyright © 2004 Omnigraphics, Inc.
ISSN 1058-2347 • ISBN 0-7808-0683-2

The information in this publication was compiled from the sources cited and from other sources considered reliable. While every possible effort has been made to ensure reliability, the publisher will not assume liability for damages caused by inaccuracies in the data, and makes no warranty, express or implied, on the accuracy of the information contained herein.

∞

This book is printed on acid-free paper meeting the ANSI Z39.48 Standard. The infinity symbol that appears above indicates that the paper in this book meets that standard.

Printed in the United States

Contents

Preface

Biography Today is a magazine designed and written for the young reader—ages 9 and above—and covers individuals that librarians and teachers tell us that young people want to know about most: entertainers, athletes, writers, illustrators, cartoonists, and political leaders.

The Plan of the Work

The publication was especially created to appeal to young readers in a format they can enjoy reading and readily understand. Each issue contains approximately 10 sketches arranged alphabetically. Each entry provides at least one picture of the individual profiled, and bold-faced rubrics lead the reader to information on birth, youth, early memories, education, first jobs, marriage and family, career highlights, memorable experiences, hobbies, and honors and awards. Each of the entries ends with a list of easily accessible sources designed to lead the student to further reading on the individual and a current address. Obituary entries are also included, written to provide a perspective on the individual's entire career. Obituaries are clearly marked in both the table of contents and at the beginning of the entry.

Biographies are prepared by Omnigraphics editors after extensive research, utilizing the most current materials available. Those sources that are generally available to students appear in the list of further reading at the end of the sketch.

Indexes

A new index now appears in all *Biography Today* publications. In an effort to make the index easier to use, we have combined the **Name** and **General Index** into one, called the **Cumulative Index**. This new index contains the names of all individuals who have appeared in *Biography Today* since the series began. The names appear in bold faced type, followed by the issue in which they appeared. The General Index also contains the occupations, nationalities, and ethnic and minority origins of individuals profiled. The General Index is cumulative, including references to all individuals who have appeared in the *Biography Today* General Series and the *Biography Today* Special Subject volumes since the series began in 1992.

In a further effort to consolidate and save space, the Birthday and Places of Birth Indexes will be appearing only in the September issue and in the Annual Cumulation.

Our Advisors

This series was reviewed by an Advisory Board comprised of librarians, children's literature specialists, and reading instructors to ensure that the concept of this publication — to provide a readable and accessible biographical magazine for young readers — was on target. They evaluated the title as it developed, and their suggestions have proved invaluable. Any errors, however, are ours alone. We'd like to list the Advisory Board members, and to thank them for their efforts.

Sandra Arden, *Retired*
Assistant Director
Troy Public Library, Troy, MI

Gail Beaver
University of Michigan School of Information
Ann Arbor, MI

Marilyn Bethel, *Retired*
Broward County Public Library System
Fort Lauderdale, FL

Nancy Bryant
Brookside School Library,
Cranbrook Educational Community
Bloomfield Hills, MI

Cindy Cares
Southfield Public Library
Southfield, MI

Linda Carpino
Detroit Public Library
Detroit, MI

Carol Doll
Wayne State University Library and Information Science Program
Detroit, MI

Helen Gregory
Grosse Pointe Public Library
Grosse Pointe, MI

Jane Klasing, *Retired*
School Board of Broward County
Fort Lauderdale, FL

Marlene Lee
Broward County Public Library System
Fort Lauderdale, FL

Sylvia Mavrogenes
Miami-Dade Public Library System
Miami, FL

Carole J. McCollough
Detroit, MI

Rosemary Orlando
St. Clair Shores Public Library
St. Clair Shores, MI

Renee Schwartz
Broward County Public Library System
Fort Lauderdale, FL

Lee Sprince
Broward West Regional Library
Fort Lauderdale, FL

Susan Stewart, *Retired*
Birney Middle School Reading
Laboratory, Southfield, MI

Ethel Stoloff, *Retired*
Birney Middle School Library
Southfield, MI

Our Advisory Board stressed to us that we should not shy away from controversial or unconventional people in our profiles, and we have tried to follow their advice. The Advisory Board also mentioned that the sketches might be useful in reluctant reader and adult literacy programs, and we would value any comments librarians might have about the suitability of our magazine for those purposes.

Your Comments Are Welcome

Our goal is to be accurate and up-to-date, to give young readers information they can learn from and enjoy. Now we want to know what you think. Take a look at this issue of *Biography Today*, on approval. Write or call me with your comments. We want to provide an excellent source of biographical information for young people. Let us know how you think we're doing.

Cherie Abbey
Managing Editor, *Biography Today*
Omnigraphics, Inc.
615 Griswold Street
Detroit, MI 48226

editor@biographytoday.com
www.biographytoday.com

Congratulations!

Congratulations to the following individuals and libraries, who are receiving a free copy of *Biography Today*, Vol. 13, No. 3 for suggesting people who appear in this issue:

Dolly Bloomquist, Roosevelt Elementary Media Center, Mankato, MN
Mary Dotts, DeWitt, MI
Blythe Enke, Salt Lake City, UT
Helen Ideno, Chicago IL

Francie Berger 1960-

American Lego Builder and Marketing Manager
First Professional Lego Builder and Designer in the
United States

BIRTH

Francie Berger was born on April 3, 1960, in Queens, a borough of New York City. Her father, Harvey Berger, was a traf-
fic manager, while her mother, Rhoda, was a medical tran-
scriptionist. Berger was three years old when her only sibling,
Adam, was born. He is now an attorney.

YOUTH

Berger was raised in the New York City borough of Queens. She began playing with Lego bricks at age three, after her parents gave her a set of the plastic interlocking building blocks. "I got my first Lego set when my brother was born," she said. "I guess my parents just wanted to keep me busy." She quickly became captivated by the toy; in fact, she would rather build a house than play house. One favorite project was when "my dad and I created this little fire truck, and I always wanted to rebuild it." She recalls this fire truck with affection because they designed it themselves; this was before Lego even sold a fire truck kit. Berger's Lego collection grew as she received more blocks for her birthday and at Hanukkah. She also picked out Lego sets to give her brother, and remembers how excited she was by a Swiss villa set she chose for her brother's birthday. Not only was it was a house set, it featured a brand new arch-shaped piece. She gave the set to him for his birthday, but now jokes that "if you ask him, he'll say he never got to play with it."

> "
>
> *"I got my first Lego set when my brother was born," Berger said. "I guess my parents just wanted to keep me busy."*
>
> "

Back in the 1960s, playing with Lego blocks could sometimes be frustrating. The Danish company first began making building blocks in 1949, but they didn't appear in the United States until 1961. When Berger was a child, there were just 200 different shapes—today there are over 2,000 —and the bricks were only available in red and white. As a result, she remembers, "I always built striped houses." As her projects grew bigger, she began writing to Lego Systems, the American maker of the blocks, to ask if she could order customized sets. The stores offered small sets of assorted bricks, but "I wanted to buy red bricks so I didn't have to build striped houses." The company said they couldn't help her, but she would occasionally write them to make other requests or suggestions.

As Berger grew older, her friends grew out of playing with Lego toys. She never did, even though her junior high friends didn't think it was very cool. "It was one of many things that set me apart," she recalled. "I was an athlete, and 'girl things' didn't interest me that much. I was the one who got a baseball mitt for my 16th birthday." She also had a newspaper route to earn extra pocket money, and played organized baseball and softball. Although there weren't many sports teams for girls in the 1970s, her high school did have a softball team and she competed as a pitcher. She still spent her free time with Lego, however, and remembers getting a Lego set to pass the time when she was hospitalized briefly at age 16.

EDUCATION

In 1978 Berger graduated from Benjamin Cardoza High School in Bayside, Queens, New York. Her mother wanted her to go to business school, "because everyone knew I would own a toy store one day." She decided to study architecture instead, since designing buildings seemed the field of study closest to her passion for Lego: "Architecture is just building bigger houses with bigger bricks." She chose Virginia Polytechnic Institute (Virginia Tech) because it offered a five-year architecture program that included an entire year's internship in a real-life setting. Another bonus was the guest lecturer program, in which architects and designers visited the university to speak about their work. During her freshman year, Berger heard a lecture by a toy designer that opened her eyes to the possibility of finding a job in the toy industry. "That was when a light bulb went off in my head, and I said to myself, 'This is where I belong.'"

— " —

Berger decided to study architecture, since designing buildings seemed the field of study closest to her passion for Lego: "Architecture is just building bigger houses with bigger bricks."

— " —

At Virginia Tech, students had the option to spend their fourth year in an off-campus internship. When it was time for her fourth year, Berger managed to get a position in New York City with that lecturer's toy company, Environmental Programs. During her internship, Berger helped work on the company's design for Johnson & Johnson's toy-of-the-month program. It was the encouragement of her mentor at Environmental Programs that led her to pursue her dream of becoming a Lego builder. She wrote letters to Lego Systems, asking about a job. She kept calling and writing until she finally got in touch with the right person and convinced him to see her. She went to their Connecticut headquarters to give them a presentation of her work. She was ready to quit school and begin working right way, but they asked her to finish school instead, then send them her résumé.

Berger returned to Virginia Tech for the final year of study for her architecture degree. She was still thinking of Lego blocks, however; for her senior project she designed a scale model of a farm using Lego bricks, with the

11

*Berger (seated at right) and other designers critique a model built
by Lego master builder Kurt Zimmerle (seated at left).*

largest buildings standing about 12 inches tall. She worked from photos
of actual farm buildings, then drew up blueprints for reproducing them in
Lego blocks. Her design had 14 buildings, including a farmhouse, cow
and horse barns, a chicken coop, a pigsty, a shed, a small tractor, and even
a little outhouse. She did not construct most of the buildings, as she
would have needed thousands of bricks to complete them all, but her detailed plans fulfilled the requirements for her project. In 1983 she graduated from Virginia Tech with her degree in architecture.

CAREER HIGHLIGHTS

Getting Her Dream Job

After college, Berger continued writing to Lego Systems, figuring they still
might need a skilled Lego builder. "I knew they had guys in Denmark who
designed huge models that were shipped all over the world. I wrote and
told them they had the bricks here, why not let me design them here?"

She sent them an updated résumé (including photos and schematics of her senior project) and then left on a cross-country tour for three months in a 1977 Volkswagen Beetle. She came back on a Wednesday, and two days later got the phone call from Lego Systems: her efforts had paid off with a job offer. "I think they had finally gotten tired of listening to me on the phone," she said. "Figured if they saw me in person, maybe they could make me go away. [They] agreed to see me in person, and they never got rid of me." Actually, landing her dream job was a matter of timing, perseverance, and tenacity, Berger added; Lego happened to be ready to start their model department in 1983, and her persistence meant she was the first person they thought to hire.

Before Berger joined the company, the American division of Lego had no builders on their staff. If they needed a Lego model for a special display, they had one made by an artist in the main office in Denmark. Then the model would have to be shipped across the Atlantic to the United States. Berger began working in Lego America's new model shop in February 1984. She began with a tour of the Lego offices in Enfield, Connecticut; when she visited the department responsible for handling public relations, everyone in the letters department knew who she was. The best part, however, was her new work area, filled with an endless supply of Lego blocks in all the colors and shapes she could want.

―――― **"** ――――

"I think they had finally gotten tired of listening to me on the phone," Berger said about her many calls to Lego. "Figured if they saw me in person, maybe they could make me go away. [They] agreed to see me in person, and they never got rid of me."

―――― **"** ――――

Berger's job started out with relatively small projects: she repaired older models that had been traveling around the country and made a few small models for display in mall stores. These models might be displayed in a store like Sears or JC Penney, which were major retailers of Lego in the 1980s. Bigger models, perhaps of animals, people, or cars, were needed for Lego displays at malls and toy trade shows (where toy makers introduce new products to prospective retailers). Later, when Lego established their own specialty stores at Minnesota's Mall of America and Florida's Disney World, Berger helped create models for permanent display in the stores.

How Professionals Build a Model

When Berger first began designing her own models for Lego, it involved lots of trial and error to make sure she produced just the right shapes, even curves. "When we build a model, we don't use any bricks that you can't buy in stores, and we don't alter them or cut them or do anything weird to them," Berger explained. It is possible to create the illusion of something round (like a head) with cube-shaped Lego blocks, but it takes careful design and practice. Eventually Berger's department adopted the technique used by the Danish modeling department, using the company's specially designed graph paper to plan their models. Like an architect's drawings, these would include a plan view, looking down from the top, and an elevation view, shown from the side.

——— " ———

When Berger first began designing her own models for Lego, it involved lots of trial and error to make sure she produced just the right shapes, even curves. "When we build a model, we don't use any bricks that you can't buy in stores, and we don't alter them or cut them or do anything weird to them," Berger explained.

——— " ———

With the new graph paper, Berger could sketch out her designs and then use them as a guide for building her projects. The "best part of the job," she said, was that with over 2,000 shapes and 20 colors, "you have all the bricks you want, in any color and any size." After constructing an unglued model, she would turn it over to one of the department's model builders. The builders would then make an exact copy of Berger's design from the ground up, gluing it as they put it together. (The modelers actually use a strong chemical solvent that fuses the plastic together, forming a stronger bond than glue.) They make it as hollow as possible, to keep it light, and once the model is completed and bonded it can be transported for display.

While this method allowed for some changes during the building, it could lead to disaster. Berger recalled one time when she was building an unglued model of a life-sized human figure some six feet high. One day a woman in Lego's public relations department was showing the design lab to a reporter; with the wave of an arm she ruined six weeks' work. (Luckily, since the model broke apart in big chunks, it only took a few days for Berger to piece it back together.) Her co-worker apologized with flowers; when

This golfer made from Lego blocks demonstrates the challenge of creating round objects with square blocks.

another gentleman in the office did the same thing, the culprit appeased her with a "gorilla-gram."

Over the next few years, Lego began hiring other designers and builders, and Berger became a supervisor in her department. First she oversaw the work of the model builders, who built projects from other people's designs. Around 1992 she was named model design supervisor, overseeing the work of other designers. The special events department grew larger, including not only model designers and builders but display designers and carpenters, who created the settings in which these marvelous Lego sculptures were presented.

Sharing Enthusiasm for Lego Worldwide

Berger's creations during her years in Lego's model design department included some amazing projects. She created a six-foot-tall pirate, complete with red beard, for a display in the famous New York City toy store F.A.O. Schwartz. The flagship Toys "R" Us store in New York's Herald

15

*Berger with her model of the U.S. Capitol building, made with
one-half million Lego blocks.*

Square once featured an animal amusement park with a six-foot Lego
roller coaster that Berger created. Minnesota's Mall of America displayed
her department's tallest work, a 24-foot-high clock tower that took four
months to create. One of her most intricate models was a copy of the U.S.
Capitol building, complete with steps and lampposts, that measured 27
feet wide and traveled the country in a special Lego exhibit of national
landmarks. It was made from half a million Lego bricks. Berger and her
fellow designers might consult photos or plans when copying a real
building, or look at storybooks when designing an elf or a pirate. One of
her favorite projects, however, came straight from imagination: a six-foot-
tall surfing hippopotamus.

While she was part of Lego's design department, Berger often traveled around the country, building models on site. The models were used to promote Lego products at stores, toy fairs, and in the company's traveling museum. She left her position as head of the model design department in 1998 to spend two years in Mexico City. There she helped Lego Mexico start their own special events department. While in Mexico, she not only planned special Lego events, she also helped create several Lego models, including some six-foot tall models of parrots, which are native to the country. Her favorite building project during her time in Mexico, however, was a version of the Aztec sun calendar that would be featured in Lego Mexico's offices. Also known as the sun stone or calendar stone, the Aztec sun calendar is one of Mexico's national symbols, with the original discovered in the main temple of the Aztec capital Tenochtitlan (now Mexico City). Filled with detailed carvings, the stone uses pictures to represent the Aztec calendar, which has 18 months of 20 days each, plus five festival days. Berger's model was 54 inches in diameter and featured many different colors.

While Berger was working for Lego Mexico, the American office underwent a corporate restructuring. In 1999 the model design department was cut from more than 50 people to 10, and later down to just four. Computers had made designing models much simpler by using a special "Legolizer" computer program. Using this program, which company staffers created themselves, a designer could create a three-dimensional (3-D) model on screen and the computer would translate it into a building plan. The plans could be sent to builders anywhere in the world, perhaps to those at the new Legoland California theme park, which opened in 1999 and has a model-building staff on hand to repair the park's numerous models and build new exhibits. So when Berger returned to the United States in 2000 she switched jobs, moving into Lego's promotional events department as an in-store project manager. "I felt I had taken it as far as I could," she said of her job as a model designer.

Moving into Marketing

Currently, Berger's new job as an in-store project manager is to develop "retail-tainment" events: hands-on events for specific retailers. For example, she might take one of Lego's newest products and develop a two-hour event for a local Toys "R" Us or Wal-Mart store to host for its customers. She also works on designing a specific look for Lego's store displays so that customers can instantly recognize the space as the "Lego section." Sometimes she travels to supervise interactive Lego events, such as the time she went to the Kennedy Space Center in Florida, where she helped visitors build the world's largest Lego space shuttle. On these trips

Berger's favorite model is this replica of Cinderella's castle at Disney World in Orlando, Florida.

she helps her audience work together to build a project, and she says "the best thing [is] coming out here and working with the kids."

Besides traveling all over the United States and Mexico, Berger has visited cities in Canada and Costa Rica, as well as a children's museum in Guatemala. Her favorite model that she made during her travels was a replica of

Cinderella's castle built at Disney World in Orlando, Florida. She built the model, which grew to be 15 feet tall, with the assistance of the park's guests, and calls it "the absolute highlight of my career here." Her current position doesn't require as much travel, but that's no sacrifice for Berger — it gives her more time to spend at home with her daughter, Seneca. Occasionally the two of them will play with Lego blocks at home, but not very often: her daughter prefers other toys. Besides, Berger says, "it's odd to have to build with a limited amount of bricks again."

Berger's unusual occupation has brought her a curious kind of notoriety. She has been profiled in newspapers, magazines, a book called *Odd Jobs,* and even on a television TV show about "Our Favorite Toys." Her job sometimes makes casual chat challenging. Answering the simple question "what do you do?" turns into a conversation stopper as everyone in the room gathers around to hear more about her work. The envy of other adults is understandable: Berger has seen her childhood dreams come true. In working for Lego, she says, "what it always comes back to is that this is fun."

> —— " ——
>
> *Berger's job sometimes makes casual chat challenging. Answering the simple question "what do you do?" turns into a conversation stopper as everyone gathers around to hear more. The envy of other adults is understandable: Berger has seen her childhood dreams come true. In working for Lego, she says, "what it always comes back to is that this is fun."*
>
> —— " ——

HOME AND FAMILY

Berger was married in 1988; her wedding invitation featured a photo of two hippos dressed as a bride and groom — made entirely of red Lego bricks and standing three feet tall. She separated from her husband in 2001, however. She has a daughter, Seneca Rasey, born in 1995, and the two of them live in Ellington, Connecticut, in an old Victorian house Berger is restoring.

HOBBIES AND OTHER INTERESTS

Berger devotes much of her free time to restoring the 1891 Victorian house where she lives. In her spare time she also enjoys creative arts like scrapbooking and photography, as well as building dollhouses and model trains. She loves to travel when she gets the chance. In the past, Berger has volunteered for literacy programs, teaching English as a second language.

FURTHER READING

Books

Schiff, Nancy Rica. *Odd Jobs: Portraits of Unusual Occupations,* 2002

Periodicals

Baltimore Sun, Apr. 9, 1995, p.J1
Chicago Tribune, May 23, 1995, p.C4
Christian Science Monitor, Dec. 2, 1997, p.16
Hartford Courant, Feb. 8, 2003, p.B3
Los Angeles Daily News, Dec. 8, 1997, p.SV3
New York Times, June 2, 1996, sec. 13CN, p.1
New Yorker, Jan. 14, 1991, p.24

Online Articles

http://www.cbsnews.com/stories/2003/02/18/earlyshow/living
/main541087.shtml
(*CBS News,* The Early Show, "Help Wanted: Lego Builders,"
Feb. 19, 2003)

Other

Phone interview with Francie Berger by Diane Telgen, conducted May 20,
2004.

ADDRESS

Francie Berger
Lego Systems, Inc.
555 Taylor Road
P.O. Box 1600
Enfield, CT 06083-1600

WORLD WIDE WEB SITE

http://www.lego.com

Orlando Bloom 1977-

English Actor
Star of the Hit Movies *Lord of the Rings*, *Pirates of the Caribbean*, and *Troy*

BIRTH

Orlando Bloom was born on January 13, 1977, in Canterbury, England, a small, historic city about 60 miles southeast of London. His mother, Sonia Copeland-Bloom, runs a language school for foreign students. Her husband, Harry Bloom, was a South African human-rights activist and writer. He died when Orlando was four. During his childhood, Orlando believed that Bloom was his father. But when he was 13, he learned that his biological father actually was Colin Stone, a writer and family friend. Bloom has one older sister, Samantha, an actress.

Bloom's unusual name was chosen by his mother, who named him after the 17th-century composer Orlando Gibbons. Bloom often has to assure people that Orlando Bloom is his real name. It's "a hard one to live up to," he said. His nickname is "Orli."

———— **"** ————

"When I realized the heroes on 'The A-Team,' 'The Fall Guy,' and 'Knight Rider' weren't real, I decided I wanted to act, because I thought I'd love to be any number of those guys," Bloom said. "I realized those larger-than-life actors that I saw on TV, in the movies, in the theater, even street performers, could be multiple characters, and I thought that was just great. You can be an action hero, you can be Jimmy Dean, you can be those characters."

———— **"** ————

YOUTH

Bloom was shaped by his arts-loving family. His mother encouraged him and his sister to enter competitions to recite poetry and Bible passages. "That's where I got a real taste for performing," he said. "I'd love to stand up and perform, and I'd do quite well." He was an imaginative boy who played pirates and other make-believe games by the hour. Watching movies like *Superman* and his favorite TV shows made him see that acting was a way to transform himself again and again. "When I realized the heroes on 'The A-Team,' 'The Fall Guy,' and 'Knight Rider' weren't real, I decided I wanted to act, because I thought I'd love to be any number of those guys," he said. "I realized those larger-than-life actors that I saw on TV, in the movies, in the theater, even street performers, could be multiple characters, and I thought that was just great. You can be an action hero, you can be Jimmy Dean, you can be those characters." He especially admired the late American actor James Dean "because he put so much passion in his work," Bloom said.

Although Bloom was eager for an acting career, his first experience on stage was far from positive. At age four, he played a monkey in a monkey suit. "It was really hot onstage," he recalled. "I itched my [bottom] and the entire audience laughed at me." It was the "worst ever," he reported. In spite of this embarrassing start, Bloom continued to perform through his childhood and teens.

Off-stage, young Bloom was "full of action and full of ideas," his mother remembered. He was physically energetic and daring and had the scars to prove it. Over the years he has broken his nose, both legs, an arm, a wrist, a finger, a toe, and his back. He has also cracked his skull three times. "I was a little bit crazy," Bloom said. "Not crazy-crazy, but I was always the first one to jump off the wall or dive into the lake, without really thinking about the consequences."

When he was nine, Bloom broke his leg skiing and had to wear a cast for a year. It caused him to go through a chubby phase. "I sat at home really depressed because I couldn't play. I was eating biscuits [cookies] and chocolate bars." Bloom said. "I was a porker." He didn't get back on track with sports until he was 16. He admitted that he "wasn't very cool" and relied on his sister to buy him clothes — often funky items from second-hand shops. Bloom had more serious challenges, too. He has dyslexia, a condition that causes him to jumble the letters in words. It makes reading difficult. "I was teased about that because I couldn't spell properly," he said.

As he reached adolescence, Bloom had to come to grips with some surprising news: he learned that Harry Bloom was not his father; instead, his father was another man. In an interview in GQ (Gentleman's Quarterly), Bloom explained. "My mom was married to one man, but I was fathered by a second. I think she was waiting for me to be old enough to understand it. But when would you tell a kid about that stuff? It's very difficult." Harry Bloom, the man he had believed was his father, was a heroic figure. He fought for equal rights for black and white people in South Africa at a time when the country's white rulers denied equal treatment for black citizens. Harry Bloom wrote important books on the subject and even went to prison for his beliefs. He died when Bloom was four. "Harry was always a role model for me," Bloom said. "My mother spoke of him so fondly." Suddenly, at age 13, Bloom was asked to accept that his biological father was a family friend, Colin Stone. A writer, Stone had served as a guardian to Bloom from the time of Harry Bloom's death. "I don't know any family that doesn't have a little story somewhere," Bloom told GQ. "Besides, if you didn't have those things in your life, you'd be so bland."

EDUCATION AND FIRST JOBS

Because of his dyslexia, "education was always a bit tricky," Bloom said. "But I got all my exams and degrees. I just had to work harder to get them." He attended St. Edmund's, a private, co-ed school in Canterbury for students from age three to age 18. The school has a strong tradition in music and performance, and Bloom acted in school plays. His former drama teacher recalled: "Even at 14 or 15 he was getting lead roles against people who were 17 or 18. It's . . . easy to think he's a good-looking chap and that's why he's getting roles in Hollywood, but he was a very good character actor."

At 16, Bloom had completed the second stage of British schooling. Rather than remain at St. Edmund's for the last two years of pre-university education, he moved to London to join Britain's National Youth Theater. After two seasons, he won a scholarship for further training at the British American Drama Academy. While there, he won a couple of small television roles. Also, his performance in a play at a small North London theater won him an agent, a professional who helps an actor find roles. When Bloom had completed his scholarship, he played the lead role in the play *A Walk in the Vienna Woods*. He also made his movie debut in *Wilde*, a film biography of Oscar Wilde, the 19th-century Irish writer. The film was critically acclaimed, and Bloom was striking in his small part as a teenaged prostitute.

> **" Bloom's former drama teacher recalled, "Even at 14 or 15 he was getting lead roles against people who were 17 or 18. It's . . . easy to think he's a good-looking chap and that's why he's getting roles in Hollywood, but he was a very good character actor." "**

Bloom was getting noticed as a promising young actor and, with the benefit of an agent, could have entered the professional world. Instead, he chose to continue his education. He was accepted into a degree program at London's Guildhall School of Music and Drama. Such acclaimed actors as Ewan McGregor and Joseph Fiennes have attended this prestigious school. "I always planned to go to drama school," Bloom said. "I suppose I could have trained in the industry more. But, instead, I chose an environment that would be more conducive to experimenting." During his three years at the Guildhall School, he acted in classics like *Twelfth Night* by William Shakespeare and *Uncle Vanya* by 19th-century Russian playwright Anton Chekov.

In 1998, Bloom had an accident that nearly ended his career and his life. While visiting some friends, he volunteered to force open the warped door to their roof terrace. The door needed to be kicked in from the outside. Bloom climbed from a window out onto a gutter — but the gutter couldn't bear his weight. It gave way, and he fell three stories to a terrace below. "I crushed one vertebra and fractured three others. The doctors thought I wouldn't walk again," Bloom said. He was offered an operation to bolt metal plates to his spine but it carried the risk of damage to his bones and nerves. Bloom decided to take the chance and hobbled out of the hospital on crutches 12 days later. For a year, he wore a brace, and with intensive rehabilitation, he taught himself to walk again.

"I was really depressed. I was in a lot of pain," Bloom recalled of his time in the hospital. "But I had this one great teacher who came to visit and said to me, 'This is going to be the making of you.' And it was." The incident helped him to refocus and to appreciate life, Bloom said: "It made me feel that every day I'm alive is an opportunity. It had a huge effect on my life, both as an actor and as a young guy just trying to get through."

Despite this difficulty, Bloom was able to finish his education. He graduated from the Guildhall School of Music and Drama in 1999, earning an honors degree.

CAREER HIGHLIGHTS

The *Lord of the Rings* Trilogy

Just days before he graduated, Bloom was handed the role of a lifetime. New Zealander film director Peter Jackson offered him the role of elf-warrior Legolas Greenleaf in his film version of the *Lord of the Rings* trilogy, which includes *The Fellowship of the Ring*, *The Two Towers*, and *The Return of the King*. The movies were based on the well-loved books written by the English author J.R.R. Tolkien, who had been a professor of medieval languages and literature at Oxford University in England. Tolkien set the stage for the trilogy and first introduced some of the characters in *The Hobbit*, published in 1937. The three books in the *Lord of the Rings* trilogy, which were originally published in the 1950s, have often been called the finest fantasy novels ever written. Together, they have sold more than 100 million copies worldwide. (For more information, see the entries on Peter Jackson in *Biography Today Performing Artists*, Vol. 2; J.R.R. Tolkien in *Biography Today*, Jan. 2002; and Elijah Wood in *Biography Today*, Apr. 2002.)

In the *Lord of the Rings*, Tolkien created a vivid ancient world complete down to its own languages. His world is populated with fantastic creatures including hobbits, dwarves, elves, orcs, and ringwraiths. Set in the mythical world of Middle-Earth, the story centers on an evil Ring of Power, which must be destroyed before it falls into the hands of the dark

Bloom as Legolas Greenleaf in the Lord of the Rings *trilogy.*

wizard Sauron. The only way to destroy the ring, however, is to throw it back into the fire where it was forged: the lava of Mount Doom in the dark lands of Mordor.

To destroy the ring, a group of nine is selected, called the "Fellowship of the Ring": the wizard Gandalf; the men Aragorn and Boromir; the elf Legolas; the dwarf Gimli; and the hobbits Frodo, Sam, Merry, and Pippin. They pledge to travel to Mordor and cast the ring into the flames of Mount Doom in order to save Middle-Earth from eternal darkness. Together, the Fellowship must overcome great obstacles and resist the power of the ring. They set out on a terrific journey of action, adventure, and heroism, as the members of the Fellowship are tested to determine their loyalty to their oath and their ability to overcome adversity in all forms.

Creating the Movies

Filming the *Lord of the Rings* trilogy represented a "first" in the industry: it was the first time three separate films would be made as one continuous production. The three films would then be released at one-year intervals, in 2001, 2002, and 2003. It was considered a very risky strategy, but it ultimately paid off. Jackson and Bloom didn't know it yet, but the films would be acclaimed by critics and wildly popular. "I remember meeting Peter Jackson when he came to see me at school and thinking this would be really amazing," Bloom said. "I could feel the mad energy and I was so excited."

Although he had planned to continue his acting training on the London stage, Bloom didn't hesitate to commit to the *Lord of the Rings*. "It wasn't like I was going to turn that down 'Oh, no, I think I'll go and do some theater,'" he said. "I was like, *'Yeah!'*" Instead of staying in London, 22-year-old Bloom found himself on the way to New Zealand in 1999 for an 18-month, three-film shoot. It was "like winning the lottery," Bloom said. "I mean, imagine being flown to this amazing country and being taught how to shoot a bow and arrow, learn to ride horses, and study swordplay — it was sick! I was pinching myself."

For the part of Legolas, dark-haired, brown-eyed Bloom had to be transformed into a blue-eyed blond with waist-length hair. He even had a specially designed wig. But in order to make it fit, Bloom had to shave part of his own hairline. Because bow and arrow are Legolas's chief weapons, he also had to get his archery skills up to speed quickly. "I found that I had a bit of a knack for it, to where I was shooting paper plates out of the sky, which is quite cool." For some scenes, though, he only had to fire an empty bow — the arrow was later added using computer graphics. He also learned to ride horseback. Luckily, the only "war wound" from the film for accident-prone Bloom was three cracked ribs when he fell from a horse.

—— **"** ——

"[It was] like winning the lottery," Bloom said about spending 18 months in New Zealand. "I mean, imagine being flown to this amazing country and being taught how to shoot a bow and arrow, learn to ride horses, and study swordplay — it was sick! I was pinching myself."

—— **"** ——

Along with the thrills and excitement of filming, Bloom found his new role as Legolas, the regal elf warrior, somewhat intimidating. "Tolkien created the elves to be these perfect beings, to bring the world forward. It's quite a responsibility to take that to the screen." Like all of the elves in the *Lord of the Rings*, Legolas is immortal. At the time of the story he is 2,931 years old. Bloom saw Legolas as something of a superhero. "Elves have this superhuman strength, yet they're so graceful. I wanted him to have a balletic movement to him. A real grace, but he's . . . a red-blooded, full-on warrior elf. The movement was more sophisticated than your average human. . . . [It] was more like a samurai," Bloom said, referring to the aristocratic Japanese warriors from around the 17th century who followed a strict code of honor.

———— **"** ————

"Tolkien created the elves to be these perfect beings, to bring the world forward. It's quite a responsibility to take that to the screen," Bloom said about Legolas, *whom he considered something of a superhero. "Elves have this superhuman strength, yet they're so graceful. I wanted him to have a balletic movement to him. A real grace, but he's . . . a red-blooded, full-on warrior elf. The movement was more sophisticated than your average human. . . . [It] was more like a samurai."*

———— **"** ————

Along with the challenge of bringing a superhuman being to life, Bloom found himself performing with superstars of the acting profession. He said: "[Can] you imagine what it was like for me, coming right out of drama school, being thrown into a group of actors like Ian McKellen, Ian Holm, and Christopher Lee. . . . Yes, it was incredibly daunting." On the other hand, Bloom said, the cast members were the ultimate teachers: "I just watched how the other actors were going about what they were doing. In a way it was perfect. It was like a continuation of school."

During the year and a half of filming, New Zealand became something of a spiritual home for Bloom, and the cast was like a family. "We all got on so well and grew close, going fishing or on road trips together during free time," he said. Bloom lived in a house next to the sea. "You could almost spit in it," he said. "The Hobbits and I went surfing all the time." The filming itself was cloaked in secrecy. "I would have to wear a hooded jacket in the car on the way to the set and home every day, too, if I still had the elf ears on," he said. According to Bloom, the only negative side to making the *Lord of the Rings* was that it had to end. He recalled the celebration the cast and crew had after the last re-shoot had been completed: "The stunt guys did a hucker, which is a Maori kind of pole dance [Maori are the native people of New Zealand]. Peter said some amazing things. It was really sad and hugely emotional."

Scenes from the Lord of the Rings *trilogy.*

Today, Bloom wears an indelible souvenir of his experience on *Lord of the Rings*. He has a tattoo on his forearm of the "elvish" symbol for nine in honor of the nine members of Tolkien's fellowship. Each of the actors who portrayed a member of the fellowship got one. Not as visible, but just as permanent, is Bloom's feeling for his character. "I hope I carry a part of [Legolas] with me forever," he said. "He's a special, special character and of course, my first. I'm never going to let go of him." Bloom also said he will never stop being grateful to Peter Jackson for the experience he gave him. "Not just as an actor but as a guy getting to live in New Zealand and experience that culture," Bloom said.

After working on *Lord of the Rings*, Bloom next went to work on *Black Hawk Down* (2001), by the established director Ridley Scott. In this film about U.S. military personnel stationed in Somalia, a country on the coast of eastern Africa, Bloom has a small role as Pfc. Todd Blackburn, a young, inexperienced U.S. Army ranger. In a case of art imitating life, his character falls 70 feet from a helicopter. He breaks his back and many other body parts. He then is taken to safety in a convoy. Bloom recalled, "After I had my fall, I was in hospital lying right next to a young soldier with a paralyzing injury. It's surreal how life has these patterns."

Pirates of the Caribbean

In 2003, Bloom appeared in another huge hit film, *Pirates of the Caribbean: the Curse of the Black Pearl*. If the *Lord of the Rings* won Bloom won female fans' attention, his appearance in *Pirates of the Caribbean* sealed their affection. Funny, rollicking, romantic, and scary all at once, the film was a huge success with audiences. Johnny Depp steals the show with his mincing, comical portrayal of scalawag pirate Capt. Jack Sparrow. But Bloom is firmly the romantic heart of the film, as earnest blacksmith Will Turner, a good-hearted lad in love with the local beauty, Elizabeth (played by Keira Knightley). He teams up with swaggering Sparrow to rescue his fair damsel.

"It's all that fun, swashbuckling stuff, which is a good laugh," Bloom said. "I loved the boat-to-boat battles and all the swinging on ropes." Co-star Geoffrey Rush, with whom he also worked in *Ned Kelly*, recommended him for the role in *Pirates*. And when Bloom heard who else was in the cast, he signed right on. "Knowing that Johnny Depp was involved in this movie made it a no-brainer for me," he said. "Johnny is such a hero of mine. As a kid, I'd run to his movies." Knightley became the envy of females everywhere when she shared Bloom's first on-screen kiss. "He has

*LEFT AND ABOVE:
Scenes from* Pirates of the
Caribbean.

BELOW: A scene from
Black Hawk Down *with
Bloom (center) as Blackburn
and Josh Hartnett (right) as
Eversmann.*

an amazing future ahead of him," she said. "He's a very good-looking boy and a lovely person. . . . I have nothing but good things to say about the kiss." The chemistry of the actors, and the liveliness of the story, won *Pirates* a huge following. The film was critically acclaimed, as well as financially successful. A hotly anticipated sequel is already in the works, in which Bloom, Depp, and Knightley return to their original roles. Filming is to begin in winter 2005.

Recent Films

Bloom appeared in several 2004 releases, both smaller films and a big blockbuster. He returned to period drama in *Ned Kelly*, set in the 19th century in the outback of Australia. The film tells the story of the real-life Australian outlaw and gang-leader Kelly, played by Heath Ledger. Bloom plays the supporting role of Irishman Joe Byrne, Kelly's best friend. Kelly and his gang create havoc in their bush community as a reaction to the abuse dished out by the local authorities. The gang "feels they are hard done by and persecuted unjustly," Bloom explained. "I have to admit, I didn't know a lot about the real-life Ned Kelly or the members of his gang. In the end, it was so rewarding playing a character who was a hero in real life to so many Australians."

> *In* Troy, *Bloom was happy to play a bad boy for a change. "Will in* Pirates *and Legolas — they're obvious hero types," he said. "Paris is an anti-hero, and this is the story of stories."*

Bloom's next release, *The Calcium Kid*, marked his first chance to take a lead role in a film. In this lower-budget British comedy, Bloom portrays a young milkman, Jimmy, who accidentally discovers he has a gift for boxing. Before he knows it, to his surprise, he is pegged to face an undefeated American champion. "Jimmy is an everyday geezer," Bloom said of his character. "He's not trying to be anything. In fact, he's just like me." The film was released in Britain in 2004 to mostly negative reviews. It reportedly will go straight to video release in the United States.

Also in 2004, Bloom appeared in the big-budget historical epic, *Troy*. The film is based on the tales related by the ancient Greek poet Homer in his epic poem *The Odyssey*. As in the *Lord of the Rings* trilogy, Bloom was part of a large, ensemble cast, including such major actors as Brad Pitt and Peter O'Toole. The director, Wolfgang Petersen, is noted for his international hit *A Perfect Storm* and earlier success, *Das Boot (The Boat)*, a

Bloom as
Paris and
Diane
Kruger as
Helen in
scenes from
Troy.

German-language film. In *Troy*, Bloom plays the pivotal role of Prince Paris. Paris is a lover more than a warrior, but when he steals the famous beauty Helen from the King of Sparta he ignites war. Bloom was happy to play a bad boy for a change. "Will in *Pirates* and Legolas—they're obvious hero types," Bloom said. "Paris is an anti-hero, and this is the story of stories." The film has received mostly positive reviews, though more for the scope and technical success of the movie than for the individual performances.

Upcoming Projects

Bloom has several new movies on the way. He has finished *Haven*, a small, independent film set in the Cayman Islands in the West Indies. Bloom portrays a happy-go-lucky British guy who gets involved with two criminals, played by Bill Paxton and Gabriel Byrne. In addition to starring in *Haven*, Bloom is the film's co-producer. "It's the first time I've done that," he said. "In terms of the role that I've been playing as a producer, it's been really just a sounding board; it's very much a collaborative effort."

——— **"** ———

"I never really wanted to be famous," Bloom said. "I trained for three years at drama school to be an actor — not a celebrity." Indeed, director Peter Jackson praises Bloom for not letting fame go to his head. "He [is] the same guy, fun-loving, enthusiastic, and supportive. He doesn't buy into the nonsense."

——— **"** ———

Currently in production is *Kingdom of Heaven*, directed by Ridley Scott, with whom Bloom previously worked on *Black Hawk Down*. The story takes place during the Crusades, a series of military campaigns that were undertaken by European Christians against Muslim powers between the 11th and 14th centuries. The invaders were trying to seize the city of Jerusalem and other Holy Lands from the Muslims. As in *Pirates of the Caribbean*, Bloom plays a blacksmith with a noble cause. His character, Balian of Ibelin, becomes a knight in order to defend Jerusalem against the Crusaders. Along the way, he saves a kingdom and falls in love with Sibylla, Princess of Jerusalem (played by Eva Green). "I swore to myself I wasn't going to do another movie with a horse and a sword, but here I am," Bloom said. "It's cool." According to Scott, the film will be produced on a scale slightly larger than *Gladiator*, his Oscar-winning epic. The much-awaited film is expected in May 2005.

Once that wraps, Bloom is set to transform himself into someone completely different: a present-day American. As the lead in *Elizabethtown*, he will portray a depressed young man returning to Kentucky for his father's funeral. Kirsten Dunst co-stars as a possible love interest. The movie has been described as a romantic comedy with strong dramatic elements. The director is Cameron Crowe, known for *Jerry Maguire* and *Almost Famous*. And of course, Bloom's many fans are also anxiously awaiting the sequel to *Pirates of the Caribbean*.

Bloom's Appeal

Since his first appearance in the *Lord of the Rings* trilogy, Bloom has won the hearts of fans. Judging from his stacks of mail, many of them are females. According to *Ned Kelly* director Gregor Jordan, "There's a reason why girls go crazy for him. He's in the long tradition of guys like James Dean and Russell Crowe. There's just something about him that makes people want to sit in the dark and watch him on a movie screen." Jerry Bruckheimer, the producer of *Pirates*, would concur. "He is so natural. He's got that look, as if he could have come from another time." Writing in *GQ*, Allison Glock also commented on Bloom's old-fashioned appeal. She wrote, "He is courtly and sweetly naive. His lithe body seems built for tights and ruffs. Even his face has the delicate features of a more civilized era."

Indeed, interviewers note that Bloom's behavior, as well as appearance, could come from another era. He has been described as soft-spoken, polite, and an attentive listener. One journalist said that he had an almost spiritual presence. Another reported that during the course of one interview, Bloom graciously gave autographs to fans and helped an elderly man whose wheelchair had broken down.

As for Bloom, he is uncomfortable with adoration and shrinks from his heart-throb status. "I never really wanted to be famous," he said. "I trained for three years at drama school to be an actor — not a celebrity." Indeed, director Peter Jackson praises him for not letting fame go to his head. "He [is] the same guy, fun-loving, enthusiastic, and supportive. He doesn't buy into the nonsense."

When it comes to making choices for his film roles, Bloom embraces Johnny Depp's advice: "Don't go for the money. Keep it real and follow your heart. Take your time." Bloom also plans not to let his status as a teen idol keep him from building a varied and challenging career. "You know the heart-throb thing — I hope that it won't stop me from making more interesting choices, because that's what I intend to try and do," he said.

HOME AND FAMILY

Bloom is often on the road filming—in Mexico, Malta, Morocco, or the Caribbean, to name only a few of his recent movie locations. When he isn't working, he divides his time between Los Angeles and London. He remains close to his mother, sister, and old friends, whom he likes to see as often as he can. He is unmarried. Currently, he is reported to be dating actress Kate Bosworth, the star of *Blue Crush*. But Bloom is adamant about keeping his private life private. "I've got a lot of love in my life and I'm happy," he said.

HOBBIES AND OTHER INTERESTS

Bloom enjoys extreme sports, including skydiving, snow boarding, surfing, and bungee jumping. "When you're in front of a 150-foot drop with a piece of cord tied to your ankles, it's scary," he said. "But you confront that fear and get over it and it empowers you." His back injury in 1998 hasn't deterred him from what he loves to do. But it has made him more cautious. "Now I approach everything in a much less flighty manner," he said. "If I'm gonna get on a snowboard, I'm aware that I could do serious damage to myself." As his career gets busier, he enjoys "down" time more. "When I'm not working I prefer to sit and do nothing," Bloom said. "Go to a beach. Go for a walk. The simple things have suddenly become more enjoyable."

Bloom is a vegetarian. He reportedly likes shopping and antiques. He has studied photography and art; if he weren't an actor, he says he'd like to be a sculptor. A music fan, he enjoys Jeff Buckley, Coldplay, Radiohead, Jack Johnson, and Kings of Leon.

FILMS

Wilde, 1997
The Lord of the Rings: The Fellowship of the Ring, 2001
Black Hawk Down, 2001
The Lord of the Rings: The Two Towers, 2002
The Lord of the Rings: The Return of the King, 2003
Pirates of the Caribbean: The Curse of the Black Pearl, 2003
Ned Kelly, 2004
The Calcium Kid, 2004 (United Kingdom release)
Troy, 2004

HONORS AND AWARDS

Best Breakthrough Star Award (MTV Movie Awards): 2002, for *Lord of the Rings: The Fellowship of the Ring*

FURTHER READING

Books

Contemporary Theatre, Film, and Television, Vol. 43, 2002

Periodicals

Houston Chronicle, July 13, 2003, p.8
Interview, Nov. 2001, p.50
Newsday, Feb. 10, 2002, p.D3
The Record (Bergen County, NJ), July 6, 2003, p.E1
Teen People, Dec. 1, 2002, p.80; Feb. 1, 2004, p.78
USA Today, July 7, 2003, p.D1
YM, June 2004, p.80

Online Databases

Biography Resource Center Online, 2004, articles from *Contemporary Theatre, Film, and Television,* 2002

ADDRESS

Orlando Bloom
International Creative Management
8942 Wilshire Blvd.
Beverly Hills, CA 90211

WORLD WIDE WEB SITES

http://www.lordoftherings.net
http://disney.go.com/disneyvideos/liveaction/pirates/main_site/main.html
http://troymovie.warnerbros.com

Carla Hayden 1952-

American Librarian
Director of the Enoch Pratt Free Library in Baltimore
and Former President of the American Library
Association

BIRTH

Carla Hayden was born in Tallahassee, Florida, on August 10,
1952. Her parents were Bruce Hayden, Jr., and Colleen (Dowl-
ing) Hayden. Her father played the violin and taught music,
while her mother played piano and later worked for the city of
Chicago.

YOUTH

Carla Hayden is a private person who rarely talks about her childhood. She was born in Tallahassee while her father was teaching at Florida A&M University, but the family soon moved to New York City so he could play with the jazz musician Cannonball Adderly. Since both of her parents were musicians, Carla grew up enjoying music. "I have fond memories of sitting under a piano reading books while my parents practiced," she recalled.

After her parents divorced, Carla moved with her mother to Chicago, where she spent most of her youth. She loved to read as a child, especially the Nancy Drew mystery series and historical romances. Her favorite book was *Bright April,* by Marguerite DeAngeli, which tells the story of a young African-American girl's first encounter with racism in her local Brownie troop. "I love it to this day," she stated. Thanks to her love of books, Carla felt drawn to the library from an early age. "I still remember the first time my mother took me to a library," she noted. "There was something magical about those books." Although the idea of becoming a librarian appealed to her, she remembered hearing her grandmother say that it could not possibly be a very exciting career choice.

— **"** —

"I still remember the first time my mother took me to a library," Hayden noted. *"There was something magical about those books."*

— **"** —

EDUCATION AND FIRST JOBS

Hayden attended Roosevelt University in Chicago. After graduating with a bachelor of arts degree in 1973, she went to work as a children's librarian in the Chicago Public Library. She was inspired by one of her colleagues there, a woman who "wore jeans, had frizzy hair, and got down on the floor to talk with kids." This woman's hands-on approach to the job convinced Hayden to build a career as a librarian. She continued her education at the University of Chicago's Graduate Library School, earning a master's degree in library science in 1977. Two years later, she was promoted to young adult services coordinator at the Chicago Public Library.

In 1982 Hayden left her job to become library services coordinator at Chicago's Museum of Science and Industry. She also began working on her Ph.D. (doctorate) in Library Science at the University of Chicago. Upon earning her doctorate in 1987, she left her job at the museum to teach at the University of Pittsburgh's School of Library and Information Science.

In May 1991 she returned to the Chicago Public Library as its first deputy commissioner and chief librarian — the library's second-highest position.

CAREER HIGHLIGHTS

Although Hayden was happy to be back working at her hometown library, she began to feel restless after spending a year as second-in-command. The library's top position was open, but the board of trustees could not seem to decide on a candidate to fill the job. Meanwhile, Hayden heard about another interesting job opening at the Enoch Pratt Free Library in Baltimore, Maryland. The Enoch Pratt was the first public library system to be established in the United States, but it had fallen on hard times due to budget cutbacks and declining circulation at many of its branches. Although Hayden had been raised and educated in Chicago, the challenge of saving an old and once-glorious library was one she could not pass up. "It was a tough decision," Hayden recalled, "but Baltimore had a real appeal to me."

Just as the board of trustees at Enoch Pratt was celebrating Hayden's decision to accept the job, Chicago Mayor Richard Daley announced that she had been appointed to the top job at the Chicago Public Library. Daley had heard that Hayden was considering a job elsewhere. He thought that if he acted quickly enough and gave her the highly paid job she had been waiting for, he could persuade her to stay. Unfortunately, Daley's announcement was released to the press without being cleared by Hayden, resulting in an embarrassing mix-up. The Chicago offer also came too late to change her mind. Hayden accepted the Enoch Pratt job and moved to Baltimore in July 1993.

A Library with a History

The Enoch Pratt Free Library was established in 1882 by Enoch Pratt, a young man from Massachusetts who had come to Baltimore as an iron merchant. Pratt soon formed his own company, E. Pratt & Bros., which became a major force in the railroad and steamboating industries as well as other business ventures. By the time he was ready to retire, Pratt was a very wealthy man who wanted to do something for the city that had provided him with so many opportunities.

Pratt gave Baltimore money to establish a central library with four branches scattered throughout the city. "My library," he said, "shall be for all, rich and poor, without distinction of race or color." Pratt made it clear that although the library system would be owned by the city of Baltimore, its operation would be guided by a board of trustees separate from city government. The

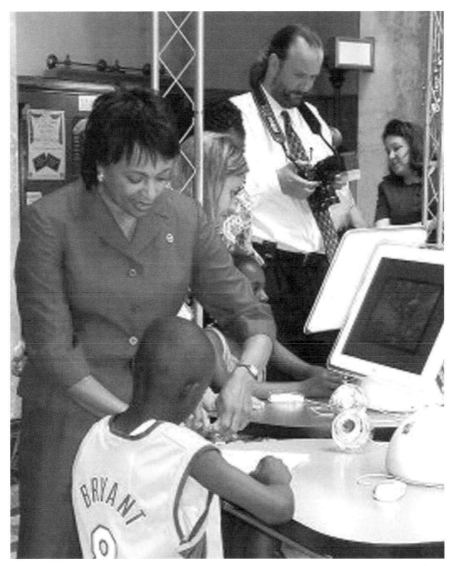

Throughout her career as a librarian, Hayden has emphasized the importance of providing resources for students.

result became a model for city public libraries throughout America. It even inspired Pittsburgh industrialist Andrew Carnegie to begin his famous library-building program in the early 20th century.

The Enoch Pratt Free Library had flourished for more than 100 years, but by the time Hayden took over it was facing some serious problems. For example, some of the 28 branch libraries were housed in 19th-century buildings that needed expensive repairs. In addition, a 30 percent decline in Baltimore's population meant that the branches in several city neighborhoods did not see much use. Finally, the city of Baltimore had not increased its contribution to the library's budget in a number of years.

Immediately after taking the director position, Hayden came up with a plan to improve the library's financial situation. She persuaded the city to increase the library's budget, and she also started raising money from grants and private sources. But Hayden knew that she would also have to make some unpopular changes. She wanted the libraries to be open on Saturdays — something that staff members often resisted. In order to afford this change, she closed the branches during "quiet times" when not many people used them. Even more controversial was her decision to close several of the branches so that the money saved could be put toward making improvements elsewhere.

According to former American Library Association President Peggy Sullivan, closing branch libraries is normally considered "the quickest way for a director to ruin his or her career." As expected, many people in Baltimore were upset about Hayden's actions, even though she emphasized that her decisions on which branches to close were made on the basis of their location, number of visitors, and the condition of their buildings. Some critics also complained that closing the branch libraries took away a "safe haven" for many of the city's children. Hayden countered some of this criticism by pointing out that the money saved would enable her to build four large regional libraries and expand the central library to make its collections more accessible to the public.

Turning the Library into a Community Resource

Once she had the library system's financial problems under control, Hayden wasted no time in reorganizing it and instituting several long-overdue changes. She created an Information Access Division to run "Sailor," an electronic network that serves public libraries and their users throughout the state of Maryland. Sailor proved extremely popular and eventually received about 30,000 hits per day. Hayden also turned the library into the city of Baltimore's electronic information provider, setting up electronic kiosks in grocery stores and malls that people could use to gain access to the library's collections.

Hayden also instituted several programs directly aimed at children and young adults. She implemented an electronic literacy program for the city's at-risk children and set up a multimedia center to provide homework as-

Hayden introduced a variety of programs for children after taking the reins at Baltimore's Enoch Pratt Free Library.

sistance, computer training, and college counseling to middle and high school students. She also replaced the library's bookmobile, which spent most of its time in the shop being repaired, with an entire fleet of vehicles that could bring books and library services to summer camps, recreation centers, day care facilities, and apartment complexes for the elderly.

Not all of Hayden's ideas have been high-tech in nature, however. For example, she used an innovative idea to eliminate security concerns at the central library. Some patrons felt uncomfortable about dropping their children off at the library because there was a soup kitchen serving homeless people across the street. Remembering Enoch Pratt's original vision of a library that is open to everyone, Hayden solved the security problem by instituting a "Coffee for Cops" program, in which local police officers could drop by any time and use a special area of the library as their "office" when they were on patrol. Parents and their children felt much more comfortable about using the library when they routinely saw police officers sitting in the facility filling out paperwork.

President of the ALA

Hayden had been an active member of the American Library Association (ALA) throughout her career. Founded in 1876, the ALA is a professional organization for librarians, with 65,000 members around the country. Her achievements as director of Enoch Pratt brought her a certain amount of renown in her field. In fact, her stature enabled her to win election as president of the ALA for 2003-2004. She became only the second African-American woman to hold the prestigious position.

—————— `` ——————

"We need to recommit ourselves to the ideal of providing equal access to everyone, anywhere, any time, and in any format, particularly those groups who are already underserved, such as residents of rural and urban America, minorities, senior citizens, and the handicapped."

—————— '' ——————

Upon assuming the presidency of the ALA on June 24, 2003, Hayden said that one of her highest priorities would be to ensure equity of access in libraries. "Equity of access is not only one of the basic tenets of our profession but it encompasses all of our basic and pressing contemporary concerns as well," said Hayden. "We need to recommit ourselves to the ideal of providing equal access to everyone, anywhere, any time, and in any format, particularly those groups who are already underserved, such as residents of rural and urban America, minorities, senior citizens, and the handicapped."

As ALA president, Hayden did not shy away from taking strong public stances on issues she thought were important. For example, she became a vocal critic of the Patriot Act, a piece of legislation passed by Congress following the terrorist attacks against the United States on September 11, 2001. The Patriot Act gave the federal government broad powers to investigate the activities of suspected terrorists. For example, it lowered the legal standards federal investigators needed to meet in order to monitor people's Internet use and cell phone conversations. The Patriot Act also allowed the U.S. government to force suspected terrorists to leave the country and to take control of money and property that might be used to finance terrorist activities.

Hayden and many fellow librarians objected to a specific provision of the Patriot Act — Section 215 — which granted federal investigators access to the library records of individual patrons. The law required libraries and

As president of the ALA, Hayden emphasized equity of access to library resources and the preservation of privacy rights.

bookstores to provide information about individuals' reading habits to government officials. But it also placed a gag order on librarians and booksellers, preventing them from publicly disclosing that they had been contacted under the Patriot Act. As the president of ALA, Hayden spoke out against the provisions of Section 215. She claimed that the law intruded on library patrons' right to privacy and prevented libraries from serving their intended function in American society. "Now, more than ever, libraries worldwide represent a calming sanctuary during tumultuous times and a place of opportunity and enjoyment," Hayden stated in *American Libraries* magazine. "Yet the unifying factor is the ability to inquire and to receive service without fear of reprisal and with a measure of privacy. When that ability is threatened, we have an obligation to question how intrusions into the basic rights of our patrons will inhibit their use and ultimately invade the public's right to know."

U.S. Attorney General John Ashcroft dismissed Hayden's criticism of the Patriot Act. He accused the ALA of exaggerating the government's interest in the library records of ordinary people. "The fact is, with just 11,000 FBI agents and over a billion visitors to America's libraries each year, the Department of Justice has neither the staffing, the time, nor the inclination to monitor the reading habits of Americans," he stated. Ashcroft also warned the ALA that their negative comments about Section 215 of the Patriot Act could trigger "baseless hysteria," a comment that angered many librarians. But he later called Hayden personally to reassure her that he would at least make public a report to Congress about how often library records were actually searched.

Another law that Hayden opposed was the Children's Internet Protection Act (CIPA). This law said that libraries that provided their patrons with Internet access were required to install filters designed to prevent school-children from accessing pornography and other inappropriate information online. Such filters did not always work properly. For example, they were criticized for occasionally restricting access to information about legitimate research topics, like breast cancer. Still, libraries that did not install the filters stood to lose government funding.

—————— " ——————

"While we face many challenges [as librarians], I see a profession that is progressively more vibrant and visible than at any time I can recall in my professional career," Hayden said. "Libraries have become so high-profile and library workers and supporters so increasingly vocal that we are making waves across the nation."

—————— " ——————

Believing that such restrictions placed an unconstitutional limit on the freedom of speech, Hayden and the ALA took the case all the way to the U.S. Supreme Court. But the Court ruled against the ALA, saying that the law was constitutional as long as the filters could be disabled upon request by adult library users. Hayden was disappointed with the Supreme Court decision, which she worried "could result in ignorance about a life-threatening disease or leave teenagers with unanswered questions about their physical and mental development." She pointed out that disabling filters is both time-consuming and expensive, and that libraries that could afford to do without government assistance would probably decide not to install the filters in the first place.

Recent Achievements

In March 2004 the Enoch Pratt Free Library opened a $15 million, four-story annex—its first major expansion after closing one-fourth of its 28 branch libraries between 1997 and 2001. The new annex is designed to give the public more access to its special collections, which include materials relating to Baltimore newspaper essayist H.L. Mencken and an exten-

Hayden celebrates with Maryland Congressman Elijah E. Cummings after she received the 2003 Ms. *magazine Woman of the Year Award.*

sive African-American collection. On a separate floor is the Maryland Reading Room, where patrons can find 19th-century books, maps, postcards, and pamphlets about the state. The annex even contains a "cybercafe," which reflects the widespread trend toward relaxing rules against bringing food and drinks into libraries. "I want very much to be a part of the story of the Enoch Pratt Free Library," Hayden stated. "I only hope I'll know when it is time for me to get off the stage."

In July 2004 Hayden completed her one-year term as president of the ALA. She was succeeded by Carol A. Brey-Casiano, executive director of the El Paso (Texas) Public Library. Upon completing her term as president, Hayden stated that her year at the organization's helm had been an uplifting and inspiring one for her personally. "While we face many challenges [as librarians], I see a profession that is progressively more vibrant and visible than at any time I can recall in my professional career," she wrote in *American Libraries.* "Libraries have become so high-profile and library workers and supporters so increasingly vocal that we are making waves across the nation. During my college and university campus visits, I became reassured about the future due to the commitment and passion of library school students. . . . I sincerely appreciate the opportunity to serve the membership and represent the Association. My faith in our work has been strengthened and reinforced. I look forward to continuing our efforts to ensure equity for everyone @ the library."

HONORS AND AWARDS

Black Achievers Award (YMCA): 1984
Librarian of the Year (*Library Journal*): 1995
Torch Bearer Award (Coalition of 100 Black Women): 1996
Andrew White Medal (Loyola College): 1997
President's Medal (Johns Hopkins University): 1998
Women of the Year (*Ms.* Magazine): 2003

FURTHER READING

Books

Notable Black American Women, 2002
Who's Who Among African-Americans, 2003

Periodicals

American Libraries, Sep. 2003, p.5; Nov. 2003, p.5; May 2004, p.5; June/July 2004, p.5
Baltimore Sun, Aug. 11, 1996, p.J1; July 20, 2001, p.B1; May 11, 2002, p.A1; Mar. 14, 2004, p.B1
Black Collegian, Oct. 2003, p.40
Christian Science Monitor, Sep. 8, 2003, p.11
Library Journal, Jan. 1996, p.36
Ms., Winter 2003/2004, p.45
Newsday, Sep. 17, 2003, p.A35

ADDRESS

Carla Hayden
Enoch Pratt Free Library
400 Cathedral Street
Baltimore, MD 21201-4484

WORLD WIDE WEB SITE

http://www.ala.org

Lindsay Lohan 1986-

American Actress
Star of *The Parent Trap, Freaky Friday,* and *Mean Girls*

BIRTH

Lindsay Morgan Lohan (pronounced *LOW-han*) was born on July 2, 1986, in Cold Spring Harbor, Long Island, New York. Her father, Michael Lohan, started out as an actor in television soap operas and is now an investment banker for film projects. Her mother, Dina Lohan, was once a dancer with New York's famous Radio City Rockettes. She later became a Wall Street analyst and now manages her daughter's acting career. Lindsay has three younger siblings: her brother Michael, two years younger; sister Aliana (known as "Allie"), eight years younger; and brother Dakota, ten years younger.

YOUTH

Lindsay Lohan has been acting since the age of three. Her career started when she became the first redheaded child ever signed to a contract by Ford Models, one of the top modeling agencies in New York. She went on to appear in around 60 television commercials for such companies as The Gap, Pizza Hut, and Duncan-Hines. Lindsay gained her first real exposure acting alongside the veteran comedian and actor Bill Cosby in a commercial for Jell-O. In 1996, at the age of ten, she won the role of Alli Fowler on the television soap opera "Another World."

———— **"** ————

"She's so not the stage mom type," said Lohan of her mother. "I was the one begging her to take me to auditions. My mom told me that the day I got a big head was the day I stopped. She wanted me to be a regular kid."

———— **"** ————

Lindsay always felt comfortable in front of the camera and found acting and modeling to be "a lot of fun." Although Dina Lohan supported her daughter's desire to act, she also tried to make sure that Lindsay kept things in perspective. "She's so not the stage mom type," Lindsay noted. "I was the one begging her to take me to auditions. My mom told me that the day I got a big head was the day I stopped. She wanted me to be a regular kid."

EDUCATION

Lindsay received her early education in the New York City public schools. When she was selected to star in *The Parent Trap* at the age of 11, however, she was forced to miss long stretches of school and received tutoring on the set. Once the filming was completed, Lindsay decided to take some time off from acting. "It was a lot all at once at that time," she acknowledged. "And after that, I kind of just wanted to be in school. I was just 12 years old, and I just wanted to be with my family and my friends."

Lindsay remained in public school until her junior year of high school. She was a straight-A student, and her favorite subjects were math and science. She was also quite popular among her classmates. "I made it a point to get along with everyone because if you're an actress, people assume that you think you're better than everyone else," she recalled. "I wanted to make sure that people had no reason to think that about me." Once Lindsay resumed her acting career, she decided to complete the last two years of her high school education through home schooling. She eventually hopes to enroll at New York University in Manhattan, where she is considering studying law.

CAREER HIGHLIGHTS

The Parent Trap

When Lohan was only 11, she landed the starring role in *The Parent Trap*, a remake of a hit Walt Disney comedy from 1961. *The Parent Trap* presented an unusually challenging acting assignment for her, because she was required to play two separate roles as a set of identical twins. The film's director, Nancy Meyer, spent a long time searching for a young actress who could duplicate the "DNA," or "Disarming Natural Ability," of Hayley Mills, the star of the original film.

More than 4,000 girls auditioned for the role, and only five were invited to Los Angeles for a screen test (a step in the audition process in which actors perform portions of their roles on film). "I had never done a screen test before," said Lohan. "In fact, I had never been to L.A. before." Meyer recalled that she and her husband, film producer Charles Shyer, were beginning to think that perhaps they would never find the right actress for the dual role. "Then I saw Lindsay's tape, and I heard the lines for the first time," Meyer said. "She did quirky things, made faces. She's animated. Brilliant, it turns out." After viewing Lohan's screen test, Meyer exclaimed, "I want that redhead!"

The Parent Trap tells the story of identical twins Hallie and Annie, whose parents divorced shortly after they were born. Their mother, a British wedding gown designer named Elizabeth (played by Natasha Richardson), then returned to her native London. Their father, an American vineyard owner named Nick (played by Dennis Quaid), returned to his home in Napa Valley, California. Since neither parent could bear to be separated from the girls — and they felt that sending young children back and forth across the ocean for visitation would be unfair — they ultimately decided that each parent would take custody of one of the twins. As a result, Annie grows up in London with their mother, while Hallie grows up in California with their father. Because of this unusual custody arrangement, neither twin is aware of the other's existence.

51

In The Parent Trap *Lohan played identical twin sisters Annie (left) and Hallie (right), who scheme to bring their divorced parents back together again.*

Years later, Hallie and Annie meet unexpectedly when their parents end up sending them to the same summer camp. The girls immediately notice their resemblance to each other. After comparing notes, they realize that they are not only sisters, but twins. Each girl longs to meet the parent she has never known, so they hatch a plan to switch identities. They decide that Annie will pretend to be Hallie and return to their father's home in California, while Hallie will pretend to be Annie and return to their mother's home in England.

The girls spend their remaining days at camp preparing themselves for the switch. Hallie must learn to speak with a British accent, for example, while Annie must drop her accent to sound more American. The girls must also master the basic facts about each other's lives. Once they leave camp, they successfully adopt each other's identities and fool their parents — though not without some awkward and comic moments. The girls finally reveal their true identities to their parents after Nick announces his engagement to a shallow and conniving younger woman. Hallie and Annie then work together on a new scheme to disrupt their father's wedding plans and rekindle the romance between their parents.

A Challenging Role

With the help of camera tricks and computerized images, Lohan played the roles of both twins·in *The Parent Trap*. When the script called for Hallie and Annie to appear in the same scene, Lohan would play one of the parts, then change her outfit and her accent and repeat the scene playing the other part. A device called an "ear wink," which allowed Lohan to hear the other twin's lines so that she could respond with the proper timing, helped make it seem like there were two different people on screen.

Lohan acknowledged the challenges of playing two people in the same film. "I didn't really have any other acting experience," she said. "They just coached me before each scene." Although she admitted that it was scary, she also claimed that it was fun. As part of her preparation for the film, Lohan watched the original 1961 movie on video. "Most of my friends had seen the Hayley Mills version on video," she noted. "But I didn't see it until after I got the role. I'm so amazed by her performance because they didn't have the technical stuff to do two of her that easily back then."

> **"**
>
> *As Lohan prepared for her dual role in* **The Parent Trap,** *she watched the original 1961 film. "Most of my friends had seen the Hayley Mills version on video," Lohan said. "But I didn't see it until after I got the role. I'm so amazed by her performance because they didn't have the technical stuff to do two of her that easily back then."*
>
> **"**

In *Variety* magazine, film critic Joe Leydon gave Lohan high praise for her performance in the roles of both Hallie and Annie. "In the dual role originally played by 15-year-old Hayley Mills, newcomer Lohan makes a thoroughly winning impression," he wrote. "With a little help from the special-effects team, she artfully sustains the illusion of two physically similar but subtly different characters. She is particularly good at expressing each twin's efforts to hide the joy she feels when finally meeting the parent she's never known."

Lohan enjoyed making the film, even though most days included eight to ten hours of filming. She has said that she learned a lot from the other ac-

Even as her show biz career began to soar, Lohan continued to pursue her studies.

tors, particularly Dennis Quaid. "He was so terrific, he really made me feel comfortable," she recalled. Lohan also enjoyed working with her brother, Michael, who had a cameo role in the film as a boy who is mistakenly sent to an all-girls camp. The Lohan family spent a great deal of time on the set during filming, and they even brought some of Lindsay's friends to Los Angeles for a visit. They ended up going a little crazy in the hotel where they were staying. "We put shaving cream all over my brother and made a big mess in the hotel room," Lohan related. "In order to get us back, he took whipped cream — it was one in the morning and my parents were sleeping — coffee, and miles of sugar and threw it on me."

Other Projects

After she completed filming for *The Parent Trap*, Lohan took a break from acting that lasted nearly three years. With her mother's support, she decided that she wanted to live a normal life and concentrate on school for a while. But Lohan eventually found that she was ready to resume her acting career. "After a while, I started to see other girls coming up, and I was like, 'I wanna do this again,'" she recalled. Lohan's return to the screen took place in the 2000 television movie *Life-Size*, in which she played a young girl whose doll (Tyra Banks) unexpectedly comes to life.

The movie was later released on home video, where it proved very popular. (For more information on Tyra Banks, see *Biography Today Performing Artists,* Vol. 2.)

Also in 2000, Lohan was cast as Bette Midler's daughter in the pilot episode of the TV sitcom "Bette." Lohan gave up her role when producers decided to move the location of filming from New York to Los Angeles, and the series was canceled a short time later. In 2002 Lohan appeared on TV once again in the Disney Channel movie *Get a Clue.*

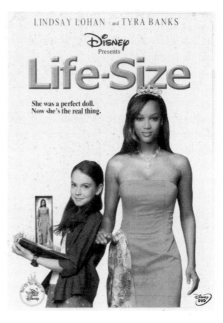

LINDSAY LOHAN and TYRA BANKS

Disney Presents

Life-Size

She was a perfect doll. Now she's the real thing.

Freaky Friday

Lohan's next big-screen opportunity came in the form of another remake of an earlier Walt Disney film, *Freaky Friday,* which was based on a 1972 novel by Mary Rodgers. The original film, released in 1976, starred a young Jodie Foster, who went on to have a successful career as an actress, director, and producer. In the remake, released in 2003, Lohan starred alongside the veteran actress Jamie Lee Curtis.

Freaky Friday tells the story of a widowed psychologist named Tess (played by Curtis) who is struggling to raise her rebellious 17-year-old daughter, Anna (played by Lohan). Although Anna is a nice girl and a good student, she manages to get on her mother's nerves by playing guitar in a garage rock band and wearing grungy clothes. At the same time, Anna feels frustrated by her mother's strict rules and conservative style. The differences between mother and daughter create a great deal of friction, particularly when Tess makes plans to remarry.

The story takes a wacky turn when Tess and Anna engage in a shouting match in a Chinese restaurant. The restaurant owner, an elderly Chinese woman with a gift for magic, decides that the mother and daughter need help to understand one another. She serves them enchanted fortune cookies that cause them to wake up the next morning—a Friday—in each other's bodies. Both are shocked and dismayed when they realize what has taken place. When Anna looks at herself in the mirror and instead sees Tess, for example, she shrieks, "I'm old! I'm like the Crypt Keeper!"

Scenes from Freaky Friday, the hit 2003 comedy starring Lohan and Jamie Lee Curtis.

Unable to find a way to switch back, the mother and daughter have no choice but to try to impersonate each other for a day. Anna goes to Tess's office and counsels her patients, for instance, while Tess goes to Anna's school and attends her classes. Many comic scenes result as mother and daughter struggle to fit in to each other's world. In the end, they both gain increased understanding and respect for the other.

Another Acting Challenge

Freaky Friday once again offered Lohan the challenge of playing two roles. First she played the role of Anna, then—once the magical switch took place—she played the role of Tess inside of Anna's body. Although Curtis faced the same challenge, Lohan claimed that her counterpart had an advantage. "Jamie had it easier than I did because she was [once] a teenager," she noted, "but I've never been an adult so I didn't have the same kind of references." To help prepare for the challenge of filming Anna as Tess and Tess as Anna, the actresses videotaped themselves doing each other's lines and actions. "That way I watched how Jamie would have done and said things and then tried to imitate that," Lohan explained.

> "*Jodie [Foster] played the daughter more as a tomboy. I play her as a punk rocker. We both rebelled but in different ways.*"

Lohan liked working with Curtis, whom she describes as "a lot of fun" and "really funny." "She is more energetic than I am," Lohan added. "She is very hyper and stuff." Curtis agreed with Lohan's assessment about which actress had the more difficult job. "It has to be believable that Lindsay's character becomes her mother," Curtis said. "I think she has the much harder job of the two of us. Lindsay has perfected the dual-role thing; she has a range that most teens never get to show."

Lohan chose not to see the original *Freaky Friday* until after she completed work on her own version. "I had never heard about this story but my mom had read the book and had seen the original movie," she noted. "She filled me in but I didn't rent the film until after we'd finished ours because that would have put too much pressure on me to be like Jodie, who is one of my acting role models." After she finally saw Foster's version, Lohan concluded that "Jodie played the daughter more as a tomboy. I play her as a punk rocker. We both rebelled but in different ways."

Lohan had to learn how to play guitar for her role in *Freaky Friday.* She was happy to have the opportunity to indulge her interest in music, including singing. "The band in the movie was made for the movie, but we had rehearsals like a real band. We would get together and go into these big rooms and play and practice our instruments together," she recalled. "I was kind of nervous, because I don't play guitar and I had to learn for the movie. Once I learned how to play it I had a lot of fun."

The fact that her first two starring roles came in remakes of Disney films does not bother Lohan. "It's great that Disney is bringing back films that our parents loved and modernizing them, especially ones that show how important strong parent and child relationships are," she stated. "It's clever marketing on Disney's behalf. Parents are the ones who buy movie tickets for their kids, and if they remember loving an old movie they're more likely to recommend it for their children." *Freaky Friday* turned out to be the surprise hit of the summer, earning more than $110 million at the box office.

———— " ————

"I was kind of nervous, because I don't play guitar and I had to learn for the movie [Freaky Friday]. *Once I learned how to play it I had a lot of fun."*

———— " ————

Grabbing New Opportunities

The success of *Freaky Friday* brought Lohan a number of additional film opportunities. In 2004 she starred as Lola in *Confessions of a Teenage Drama Queen,* based on a popular novel of the same name by Dyan Sheldon. Lola is a sophisticated New York teenager who rebels against her divorced mother's decision to relocate to the boring New Jersey suburb of Dellwood. She struggles to fit in at her new school and ends up feuding with her rich and nasty classmate Carla. *Confessions* received mostly negative reviews upon its release and did not perform very well at the box office.

Lohan experienced greater success with her second film of 2004, *Mean Girls.* Lohan starred as Cady Heron, an American teenager who has spent most of her childhood being home-schooled in Africa by her parents, who were working there as researchers. Upon returning to the United States, Cady is suddenly plunged into the pettiness of a suburban Illinois high school. "What follows is an anthropological dissection of contemporary high school culture—its norms and traditions, its food chain and battlegrounds—with the villains [of the title] proving that the lions of the Serengeti have nothing on teenage girls," wrote Lynda Obst in *Interview.*

In this scene from Mean Girls *set in the dreaded school cafeteria, Cady confronts the "Plastics": (from left) Amanda Seyfried, Rachel MacAdams, and Lacey Chabert.*

The screenplay for the movie had an interesting origin. It was written by Tina Fey, the head writer for the NBC skit comedy show "Saturday Night Live." Fey based the screenplay on the best-selling nonfiction book *Queen Bees and Wannabes: Helping Your Daughter Survive Cliques, Gossip, Boyfriends, and Other Realities of Adolescence* by Rosalind Wiseman. (For more information on Fey, see *Biography Today Authors,* Vol. 16.)

In *Mean Girls*, Cady sets out to fight the group of shallow girls known as the "Plastics" who rule the school, but she soon finds herself being drawn into their social circle instead. Fey appears in the movie as a math teacher who observes Cady's transformation from a thoughtful and caring friend into a social climber. In the end, she lectures Cady and the other female students about their tendency to be mean to one another. "Calling somebody else fat will not make you any thinner," she declares. "Calling somebody else stupid will not make you any smarter. And you've got to stop calling each other sluts and whores. It just makes it all right for guys to call you that." *Mean Girls* received generally positive reviews and opened in the No. 1 spot at the box office. Writing in *People*, Leah Rozen called the movie "a superior teen comedy with solid performances by its mostly young cast."

Lohan is scheduled to appear in several other films in late 2004 and 2005. In *Dramarama*, for example, she will play a promising drama student who is forced to transfer from her comfortable private school to a rundown public school. Since the new school has no drama program, she and a gang of misfits create their own drama club. They eventually face her old private school classmates in a drama competition. Lohan is also expected to star as Blair Waldorf in *Gossip Girl,* based on the popular book series of the same name by Cecily von Ziegesar. Finally, she will appear in a remake of the classic Disney movie *Herbie the Love Bug,* called *Herbie: Fully Loaded.*

——— **"** ———

"I want to find something different from what I usually do [in future film roles]," said Lohan. *"I don't want to give an image of doing only teen movies and just being this perfect teen. I just want to do something completely different and really rock at it."*

——— **"** ———

Spreading Her Wings

Lohan hopes that her successful movie career will lead to an additional career as a singer. "I started taking voice lessons when I was little," she explained. "I've always wanted to be an overall entertainer who sings, dances, and acts." Lohan has already contributed vocals to the soundtracks for two of her films—*Freaky Friday* and *Confessions of a Teenage Drama Queen.* In 2004 she signed a multi-album contract with Tommy Mottola's Casablanca Records.

In addition to her movies and her fledgling musical career, Lohan has appeared on the cover of numerous magazines and hosted several high-profile awards shows on television. She is seen in public so frequently that she has gained a reputation as a "party girl." Though she admits that she enjoys going to Hollywood clubs with her friends, she insists that she would never do anything to embarrass herself. "When we go out, we just get a table and observe what goes on. We're calm. We know our place. We don't have to get stupid and drunk—we can have fun without drinking," she stated. "I don't want to have a drink and have someone whip out a camera phone and [send the picture to] Disney. It's not worth it! I don't want to risk my career. . . . But it's hard being 17 years old and not being able to do the things that other 17-year-olds do, like going out, learning about yourself, finding out who you are."

As she evaluates future film projects, Lohan is interested in moving away from her "teen queen" image and taking on roles that will show a different side of her abilities. "I want to act more. I want to really act in a film and commit to something and be a different person. I mean, the characters I've played so far are very similar to who I am, so it's hard to say that I'm actually fully acting. I want to find something different from what I usually do. I don't want to give an image of doing only teen movies and just being this perfect teen," she stated. "I just want to do something completely different and really rock at it. You can only do the same thing for so long."

Lohan also hopes eventually to move beyond acting into different aspects of the film industry, including producing and directing. "Getting this sort of respect and all these opportunities at my age is incredible," she noted. "I've been talking to my friends at MTV about some ideas for shows. And I want to get into producing movies, too. If I have the skills to do something, I don't think my age should stop me."

HOME AND FAMILY

Although Lohan recently moved into her own apartment in Los Angeles, she remains very close to her family. "I was raised by an amazing family, and I think that they've kept me grounded my whole life," she noted. "My mom and I are really close, which I think is cool. If I didn't confide in her it would be stupid because she knows what I do anyway." Her mother manages her career, while her brothers and sister often appear as extras in her movies.

Still, Lohan's family has been the subject of negative articles in the press. Rumors have surfaced numerous times about trouble in her parents' marriage. Her father was arrested for assault in the spring of 2004 following a brawl at the family home. This legal problem brought attention to his past record, which included serving a four-year prison term for securities fraud. Lohan refused to comment on her father's actions except to express continued support and admiration for him.

Lohan does not have a steady boyfriend, although she has been linked romantically to several famous young men, including singer Aaron Carter and actor Wilmer Valderrama.

HOBBIES AND OTHER INTERESTS

Lohan has a dog, a miniature bichon frise named Max, and enjoys listening to music by such artists as Avril Lavigne and Eminem. She has her driver's license and has just made her first big purchase — a pre-owned BMW 330 CI convertible. She said it took a lot to persuade her mother to let her buy the luxury car. In her spare time, she enjoys swimming, ice skating, in-line skating, gymnastics, singing, reading, writing, and shopping.

HONORS AND AWARDS

Young Artist Award: 1998, for *The Parent Trap*, for Best Leading Young
    Actress in a Feature Film
MTV Movie Award: 2004, for *Freaky Friday*, for Breakthrough Female

CREDITS

Films

The Parent Trap, 1998
Freaky Friday, 2003
Confessions of a Teenage Drama Queen, 2004
Mean Girls, 2004

Television

"Another World," 1996 (TV Series)
Life-Size, 2000 (TV Movie)
"Bette," 2000 (TV Series)
Get a Clue, 2002 (TV Movie)

FURTHER READING

Books

Contemporary Theatre, Film, and Television, Vol. 55, 2004

Periodicals

Entertainment Weekly, May 7, 2004, p.57
Interview, June 2004, p.88

Los Angeles Times, Apr. 18, 2004, p.E1
Newsday, Aug. 6, 1998, p.B3; Aug. 13, 2003, p.B12
People, May 10, 2004, p.31; May 24, 2004, p.79
Seventeen, June 2004, p.123
Variety, July 27, 1998, p.51; July 28, 2003, p.27; Feb. 23, 2004, p.34
YM, Aug. 2004, p.103

ADDRESS

Lindsay Lohan
Endeavor Agency
9701 Wilshire Boulevard
10th Floor
Beverly Hills, CA 90212

WORLD WIDE WEB SITES

http://llrocks.com
http://www.meangirlsmovie.com
http://disneyvideos.disney.go.com

OUTKAST

Antwan Patton (Big Boi) 1975-
André Benjamin (André 3000) 1975-

American Hip-Hop Duo

BIRTH

The music group OutKast includes two members: Antwan Patton (Big Boi) and André Benjamin (André 3000, or sometimes just Dré). Patton was born on February 1, 1975, in Savannah, Georgia. His parents were Tony Kearse, a Marine Corps sergeant, and Rowena Patton, a retail supervisor. Benjamin was born on May 27, 1975, in Atlanta, Georgia. His parents were Lawrence Walker, a collections agent, and Sharon Benjamin, a real estate agent.

YOUTH AND EDUCATION

Both Patton and Benjamin grew up in Georgia in families that were struggling. Patton, the oldest of five children, started out in Savannah. The family moved around a lot while he was growing up, and they relocated to Atlanta when he was a teenager. Some reports say that Patton spent some time living with various family members. Benjamin, an only child, grew up in a single-parent home. He was raised by his mother, and together they lived in a series of places around southwest Atlanta until Benjamin was 15, when he made the decision to move in with his father. Despite their different family arrangements, Patton and Benjamin would soon find out that their early environments gave them much in common. "We came from basically the same background. We grew up the same way, and were into a lot of the same things," Benjamin once recalled.

> *Patton and Benjamin were both decent students, but until they met, neither gave serious consideration to a life in music. "I wanted to be a child psychologist or play football," Patton recalled. "I thought I'd be an architect, but I didn't like math," Benjamin added.*

Patton and Benjamin each attended Tri-Cities High School in the Atlanta suburb of East Point. The school had an excellent reputation for producing talented musicians: the members of the popular R&B groups TLC and Xscape had also attended Tri-Cities High. Patton and Benjamin met in 1990 at a local mall and soon found that they had similar tastes in music, including Sly and the Family Stone, James Brown, Jimi Hendrix, Prince, Parliament/Funkadelic, and popular hip-hop artists. They also found that they had similar tastes in fashion, which would seem to be in direct contrast with the image they would later cultivate. "We were preps," Patton recalled. "We wore loafers, argyle socks, and V-neck sweaters with T-shirts. We were new to the school and we didn't know anybody." The pair became friends immediately. They worked on rhymes together and also developed their individual styles by having rhyming competitions in their school cafeteria.

Patton and Benjamin were both decent students, but until they met, neither gave serious consideration to a life in music. "I wanted to be a child psychologist or play football," Patton recalled. "I thought I'd be an architect, but I didn't like math," Benjamin added. But once the duo had legitimate careers in music ahead of them, they felt that their studies were less important. In his junior year, Benjamin dropped out a few credits short of his graduation requirements, but Patton was adamant about finishing high school and getting his diploma. "Right up until we got signed by LaFace Records, there were times when all we did was hang out," he once said. "I had been going to school for 11 years, had a 3.68 GPA and college plans, yet was on the verge of dropping out. I finally realized that school was something I needed just as much as music, and I didn't want not having a certain piece of paper to hold me back." Patton graduated on time from Tri-Cities in 1993, while Benjamin eventually went to night school to earn his diploma.

Patton later credited his high school years for being an important part of his career path. "Education is the foundation of my rhyme," he remarked. "All the things I say, all the words, came from English and science class. I like words. All I got come from words! The more words you learn the more rhymes you have!" The duo later wrote a song entitled "Git Up, Git Out," which urged their younger fans to stay in school and make the right choices.

> "
>
> *"Right up until we got signed by LaFace Records, there were times when all we did was hang out," Patton once said. "I had been going to school for 11 years, had a 3.68 GPA and college plans, yet was on the verge of dropping out. I finally realized that school was something I needed just as much as music, and I didn't want not having a certain piece of paper to hold me back."*
>
> "

CAREER HIGHLIGHTS

Getting Their Big Break

While they were still in high school, Patton and Benjamin met record producer Rico Wade through one of Patton's ex-girlfriends. Wade was a member of the Organized Noize production team, which worked with the artists TLC and En Vogue. Wade was also an accomplished musician with

expertise in the areas of keyboard samples and drum machines. The duo immediately impressed him with their rapping abilities, and he invited them to his studio. "I was in awe," Wade said. "I closed the store, we got in my Blazer and went straight to the [studio]." The three hit it off, as Benjamin later recalled. "From the first time Rico pressed 'play' on the tape, we knew we had our producer, because the beats were like nothing I had ever heard before."

Wade and Organized Noize had a studio called the Dungeon in the basement of an old house. The Dungeon attracted a lot of aspiring performers, and competition there was tough. "The basement wasn't finished," Patton recalled. "We have red clay in Georgia, so the beat machines had dust on 'em. There were old broke-up patio chairs. You had several people sitting on steps with their notebooks out. Guys sleeping upstairs on a hardwood floor. . . . We'd walk up to this deli inside a gas station and order the spaghetti special, because it came with five meatballs, so we could split it."

Organized Noize gave the duo their first break when they were invited to contribute a single to a Christmas album. At first, Patton and Benjamin were not very eager to record a Christmas song. "But we decided to do it Dungeon-style," Patton said, "a song where there's no tree, no gifts, barely a jug of eggnog." Their debut single "Player's Ball," about life on the streets, eventually went gold. They even got to record a video for the song — directed by the young up-and-comer Sean Puffy Combs.

By 1993, the duo had tried several different names for their act — including 2 Shades Deep and the Misfits — before deciding on OutKast. A pivotal moment in their careers occurred when they auditioned for record executive Antonio "LA" Reid, who at that time was president of LaFace Records. Reid wanted to sign OutKast to a contract. "Our parents wouldn't let us sign," Benjamin recalled. "We were 17. We had to wait a year. They didn't believe in rap." It was also around this time that Patton and Benjamin started using the names Big Boi and André 3000, respectively. Patton later recalled how their combination of good fortune and determination paid off. "We were lucky, no question," he admitted. "But we didn't sleep on the opportunity — every time we had a chance, we knew it, we stepped up and delivered."

Early Albums

In 1994, OutKast released its first album, *Southernplayalisticadillacmuzik*. While the CD contained two versions of "Player's Ball," Patton was quick to point out that the duo had more to say than just the themes addressed in their initial single. "A lot of people got the message of our first album mixed up," he remarked. "They just heard 'Player's Ball' and thought it was all about the pimps, the cars, and all that mess." Still, "Player's Ball" was eventually re-released as a single and went gold, selling over a half-million copies. In addition, it was Billboard's No. 1 song on the Rap Chart for six consecutive weeks. The album as a whole received praise for its casual funk, live instruments, and creative and raw grooves, all reminiscent of 1970s soul. With this commercial and critical success, OutKast set the stage for the group's later albums and gained more creative control on their next release.

By 1996, OutKast was putting the finishing touches on their second album, *ATLiens*. While the duo again worked with the Organized Noize production team, Patton and Benjamin also received producer credits on the album. The title of the record was a combination of the abbreviations for Atlanta and the word "aliens." Bubbling with originality, the album has been described as futuristic, haunting, and hypnotic.

ATLiens was considered a great leap forward for the duo, and it represented a departure in hip-hop. Unlike many of their hip-hop peers who sampled existing songs in their entirety for their own tunes, OutKast featured live instruments on many of the tracks. "While everyone else is content to steal an old hit song and add a new rap verse over it, we always start from scratch," Patton explained. "Picasso had plenty of influences, but you'd never catch him trying to remake another artist's work in the exact same way. We feel the same." Benjamin later recalled his feelings regarding the situation. "When we came up, everybody was playing straight beat machines and nobody was playing instruments like they did in my mama and them's generation. People are just starting to get back into that, and we have to research to find out about the blues, rock 'n' roll, progressive rock, calypso, reggae, jazz—anything we can learn from. If you listen to hip-hop all day long, all you're going to know is hip-hop. But if you listen more, you can mix things up to create another type of music." *ATLiens* proved to be another successful project for the duo, selling in excess of 1.5 million copies. The song "Elevators" was released as a single and became a No. 1 hit.

More Success Leads to Trouble with an American Icon

OutKast's third album, *Aquemini,* was released in 1998. The title was meant to convey a combination of the zodiac signs Aquarius (Patton) and Gemini (Benjamin). "It's simply that two people can come together as one and create," Benjamin explained. "Balance is the key. Balance in the music and balance with me and Dré," Patton added. While their partnership remained strong, the pair still maintained separate and original identities. Benjamin was starting to garner a lot of attention for his outlandish clothes, while Patton stayed true to his roots. "I'm more street, hard-core hip-hop, and Dre's more extraterrestrial," he explained. "Dré looks like the music and I look like the message." The pair even had lifestyles that were totally opposite. But *Aquemini* proved that their partnership was indeed intact, as the duo co-produced nine of the album's 14 tracks.

> **By 1998, Benjamin was starting to garner a lot of attention for his outlandish clothes, while Patton stayed true to his roots. "I'm more street, hard-core hip-hop, and Dre's more extraterrestrial," Patton explained. "Dré looks like the music and I look like the message."**

Aquemini proved to be OutKast's most diverse offering yet, complete with a star-studded lineup of guest stars including Erykah Badu, George Clinton, and members of the WuTang Clan and Goodie Mob. While the funk influence still predominated, the mix was expanded to include reggae, jazz, and world music. The album featured a number of strong tracks, including "Return of the G" and "Skew It on the Bar-B," but it was the song "Rosa Parks" that grabbed headlines. The tune, which aside from the title never mentions the famed civil rights activist by name, was OutKast's way of identifying with those who stand up for their beliefs. "When we were making the album, the music that was out at the time was not very creative. We refused to go with the flow. We wanted to be like Rosa Parks and do the opposite of what everybody else was doing. She refused to go to the back of the bus."

OutKast performing at the American Music Awards in January 2001.

While OutKast intended the song as a tribute to Parks, she was not flattered by the honor of having her name used as the title of their song. "You have her name associated with lyrics that contain vulgarity and profanity and she does not appreciate it," her attorney Gregory Reed explained. In 1999, Parks filed a lawsuit seeking $25,000 in damages for using her name without permission, claiming that the song violated her trademark rights and defamed her. In addition, she asked that her name be removed from all OutKast products. Patton and Benjamin were shocked at the actions of someone that they considered a role model. "Rosa Parks has inspired our music and our lives since we were children," they explained in a prepared statement released to the press.

OutKast won the first legal round when a federal court judge ruled that OutKast's right to use Rosa Parks's name was guaranteed by the right to free speech. At that point, the court decided that OutKast did not defame Parks. But her attorneys appealed the decision. "We won the first decision, so they're appealing it," Patton later explained. "But everybody knows that there was never any disrespect meant at all. If you know anything about OutKast — if you listen to the song — it's not about Rosa Parks. When we sing 'everybody move to the back of the bus,' we're just using that as symbolism." In 2003, the case reached the United States Court of Appeals, where OutKast argued that the song wasn't false advertising, that it didn't violate her public name, and that Parks should not have the right to sue. But OutKast lost that round — Court of Appeals decided that Parks did have the right to sue, and the Supreme Court later upheld that decision. By mid-2004, a trial date had been set for early 2005; the lawsuit had been winding its way through the courts for five years and was still unresolved.

———— " ————

"In rap, there's nothing new under the sun," Benjamin explained. "But I think it's the way you say it and how you approach it. People are afraid to step out. There's a formula to making music now, and no one really has the courage to do their own thing."

———— " ————

When all was said and done, *Aquemini* was a solid success for OutKast, selling in excess of two million copies and earning several Grammy nominations in the process. The duo later went on a successful concert tour to promote the record, opening many dates for rap superstar Lauryn Hill.

Moving into New Territory

For their next release, *Stankonia* (2000), OutKast continued to push the boundaries in their music and their message. The album combined stories about life on the streets with funk, rock, and hip-hop, seasoned with heavy doses of rhythm. "In rap, there's nothing new under the sun," Benjamin explained. "But I think it's the way you say it and how you approach it. People are afraid to step out. There's a formula to making music now, and no one really has the courage to do their own thing." Patton went on to say "It's an experimental thing. I've met a lot of producers who know exactly what they're looking for. It's like etched in stone before they begin. But we start with one element and build on to it until we get to a point where we say, 'Yeah, that's it. That's jammin.'"

Indeed, the tracks contained on OutKast's fourth release backed up Benjamin's claims. "B.O.B. (Bombs Over Baghdad)" combined social criticism with the intense rhythm of drum-and-bass dance music. As the album's first single and one of its most exciting songs, "B.O.B. (Bombs Over Baghdad)" quickly grabbed listeners' attention. The moving "Ms. Jackson"

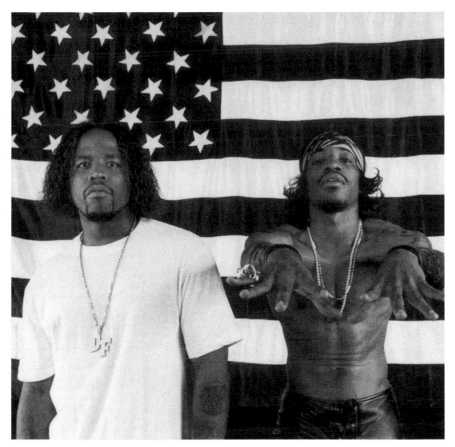

The cover of the CD Stankonia.

was an open letter to the grandmother of Benjamin's son proclaiming that he would always be a loving and responsible father. It later went on to become a No. 1 single on the pop music charts. "Toilet Tisha" was a dramatic track about a 14-year-old girl killing her newborn child. Benjamin later explained that the album's title was meant to convey a broad range of messages. "*Stankonia* is this place I imagined where you can open yourself up and be free to express anything," he said. Patton had his own interpretation of the album's mood. "*Stankonia* is where you can get butt-naked in your mind. It's the spiritual feeling where you can do whatever you want and not care what anybody else is going to say."

Stankonia was another smash hit for OutKast, selling in excess of five million copies. It impressed both fans and critics, appearing on many music critics' lists of the best albums of the year. It also won Grammy Awards for

Big Boi and André 3000 enjoy an exuberant performance at the 2004 Soul Train Music Awards.

Best Rap Performance by a Duo or Group (for "Ms. Jackson") and Best Rap Album. In addition, the record was nominated for Album of the Year and Record of the Year. But success was only part of the reward for the duo. "We decided early on that money couldn't be the motivation," Patton stated. "The motivation had to be in the love for music. We knew we wanted to be experimental, but at the same time, keep in touch with what's going on with the people. We wanted to take risks, and introduce people to something fresh."

The following year, the duo released a compilation album entitled *Big Boi and Dré Present . . . OutKast* (2001), which included the group's greatest hits as well as several rare, unreleased tracks. The collection served to document OutKast's growth over their first four albums. By this point, Patton and Benjamin had established their talent for smart, funny, and joyous funk mixed with jazz, blues, soul, R&B, rock, and world music. In many ways, their music seemed to defy musical conventions. With their continued experimentation on each new album, they had become known for their adventurous and inventive music that still claimed a retro feel. Over the years, they managed to make unconventional and ambitious music that was, at the same time, very popular. "It's this combination of eclecticism and accessibility that's made OutKast one of hip-hop's most unique forces," Lorraine Ali wrote in *Newsweek*. "The Atlanta duo mixes old and new musical styles — funk, R&B, hip-hop, rock — and ties them all together with organic jams, head-bopping rhythms, and improvisational rhymes. OutKast's cut-and-paste approach has garnered the respect of finicky underground musicians, while their chart-smart beats won over rap's mainstream crowd."

By this point, the two members of OutKast had also firmly established their separate identities. Some have called the two musicians the poet and the player. Benjamin was considered more cerebral, worried about social issues and the well-being of the community. He often brought a more futuristic and experimental flavor to the musical mix. Patton, on the other hand, was considered more of a gangster, concerned with more immediate issues like women and partying. His musical influences were more firmly based in the rap and hip-hop traditions. Yet despite their differences, both were firmly committed to the partnership.

> "We decided early on that money couldn't be the motivation," Patton stated. "The motivation had to be in the love for music. We knew we wanted to be experimental, but at the same time, keep in touch with what's going on with the people. We wanted to take risks, and introduce people to something fresh."

Speakerboxxx/The Love Below

In 2003, OutKast released a double-disc set entitled *Speakerboxxx/The Love Below*. Like all of OutKast's work, this album was full of stylistic surprises. It was essentially two solo records in the form of one double album. *Speakerboxxx*, which contained Patton's material, was an eclectic hip-hop mix with intense and fluid tracks filled with bass, electronics, and fast-paced raps. The blend of hard-edged gangster beats and bouncy party cuts proved to many that Patton was one of the smoothest and funniest rappers around. *The Love Below*, which contained Benjamin's work, was a concept album about relationships that told a series of love stories using hip-hop, jazz, funk, and R&B influences. Called irreverent, incisive, exhilarating, and experimental, *The Love Below* was also proclaimed one of the most adventurous albums of the year. "Rather than an outright collaboration, it's a two-disc set," Allison Samuels wrote in *Newsweek*, "the first all by the more mainstream Big Boi, the second all by the more experimental André. If Big Boi is red beans and rice — you can hear the influence of gospel, funk, even Jimi Hendrix — André is a crazy

The hit album Speakerboxxx/The Love Below *includes separate disks from Big Boi and André 3000.*

organic salad. . . . André is all about emotional turmoil — he still seems to be hurting over his breakup with Badu — while Big Boi is the practical-minded hedonist. . . . Taken together, the discs complement each other. But they could just have easily been solo albums."

The news of two individual albums shocked the duo's longtime fans, who worried that the release signaled the beginning of the end for OutKast. But both Benjamin and Patton were quick to put a stop to those rumors. "There is some distance," Benjamin explained. "We may venture out and do other things, but we always give each other blessings. We will always be OutKast." Still, the rumors continued to persist, especially after Benjamin declared that he had no intention to tour in support of the record. Patton took that news in stride. "If he decides not to tour, it's all good," Patton remarked. "He knows I'm going to go on the road. Ain't nothing better than the crowd's reaction to new music. We've got six albums worth of material. That's plenty to work with."

The first single was the double-sided "The Way You Move/Hey Ya!" Together, the two songs dominated the pop charts for nine weeks. "The Way You Move,"from Patton's *Speakerboxxx*, was a bass-and-horn-driven track with an old-school R&B feel to it. Some have called it an instant R&B classic. The track "Hey Ya!" from Benjamin's *The Love Below*, had a more melodic feel; it proved to be the album's breakout hit.

Many said that "Hey Ya!" invoked memories of the Beatles, a connection that the singer didn't really understand. "People say 'Hey Ya!' sounds like the Beatles, or Ike Turner, or Cheap Trick, but I have no idea where that comes from," he remarked. "I've heard of those artists, but I'm not really hip to them. When you're in the studio, you're not really thinking about breaking barriers. You just think about writing the song." Of course, the video reinforced the connection to the Beatles, with a stage set that reminded many of the band's first appearances on "The Ed Sullivan Show." What many people did not know, however, was that the song "Hey Ya!" was nearly five years old—it was originally called "Thank God for Mom and Dad" and was slated for inclusion on *Stankonia*. Benjamin later recalled its evolution, stating that the song was influenced more by punk rock than by groups like the Beatles. "I started writing that song five or six years ago. That's when my friends started hipping me to the Ramones, the Buzzcocks, the Smiths, bands like that. I was getting to this music late," he explained. "The 'Hey Ya!' chords were the first guitar chords I ever learned."

———— **"** ————

"Rather than an outright collaboration, it's a two-disc set, the first all by the more mainstream Big Boi, the second all by the more experimental André," Allison Samuels *wrote in* Newsweek. *"If Big Boi is red beans and rice—you can hear the influence of gospel, funk, even Jimi Hendrix—André is a crazy organic salad. . . . André is all about emotional turmoil—he still seems to be hurting over his breakup with Badu—while Big Boi is the practical-minded hedonist. . . . Taken together, the discs complement each other. But they could just have easily been solo albums."*

———— **"** ————

"Hey Ya!" was that rare song that appealed to a wide range of music fans, including those who loved hip-hop, rock and roll, and Top 40. As the song became more and more popular, Benjamin became more and more surprised by its success. "People think it's a light song, but the lyrics are pretty serious," he said. "It's talking about the difficulty of relationships trying to stay together. But people just want to dance to it—even older people like it."

Recognition and Success

Speakerboxxx/The Love Below was another multi-million selling success for OutKast and was the No. 1 album for seven straight weeks. For over two months, "Hey Ya!" and "The Way You Move" were the top two singles on the pop chart, making OutKast the first group to achieve such a feat since the Bee Gees back in 1978. The set went on to sell over eight million copies.

> ———— **"** ————
>
> *"It's this combination of eclecticism and accessibility that's made OutKast one of hip-hop's most unique forces," Lorraine Ali wrote in* Newsweek. *"The Atlanta duo mixes old and new musical styles—funk, R&B, hip-hop, rock—and ties them all together with organic jams, head-bopping rhythms, and improvisational rhymes. OutKast's cut-and-paste approach has garnered the respect of finicky underground musicians, while their chart-smart beats won over rap's mainstream crowd."*
>
> ———— **"** ————

Speakerboxxx/The Love Below also received six Grammy nominations. When the awards were announced on February 8, 2004, OutKast took home three trophies: Album of the Year, Best Rap Album, and Best Urban/Alternative Performance. About the only surprise of the evening came when "Hey Ya!" lost Record of the Year to Coldplay's "Clocks." Benjamin admitted that he was shocked about the way the whole evening turned out. "I thought we'd win that many awards, but not in those categories. I thought 'Hey Ya!' would get Record of the Year. When Coldplay won, I was like 'Oh really?'"

Benjamin later recalled the importance of the evening. "The best moment was when we won Album of the Year and Big Boi gave me a hug," he recalled. "The embrace lasted five—eight, nine—no maybe 15 seconds. *The Love Below* was originally supposed to be a solo album. At the last minute, management and the record company said it wasn't a good time to do that so Big Boi did *Speakerboxxx*. But I was taking so long to finish *The Love Below* that he wanted to release that as a solo album. A lot of people don't know the album almost wasn't made. So there were a lot of emotions in those seconds."

Despite the happiness surrounding their success, OutKast still managed to generate controversy on their big night. During a performance of "Hey Ya!" Benjamin and several dancers pranced around a tepee dressed in feathers, fringe, and war paint. The San Francisco-based Native American Cultural Center called the performance racist and urged a boycott of CBS (the network that broadcast

Big Boi and André 3000 pose with their three Grammy Awards, February 2004.

the event); OutKast; their record company, Arista; and the National Academy of Recording Arts and Sciences, which sponsors the Grammy Awards. The Native American Cultural Center also filed a complaint with the Federal Communications Commission (FCC). While OutKast had no comment about the situation, CBS was quick to apologize. "We are very sorry if anyone was offended," said CBS spokeswoman Nancy Carr.

Their successful double album might lead to other projects as well. OutKast plans to make a film together for Home Box Office (HBO), using cuts from *Speakerboxxx/The Love Below* and OutKast's next album as the movie's soundtrack. Patton was quick to point out that the project was not going to be autobiographical. "It's set in the Thirties, during Prohibition," he explained.

Sticking Together or Growing Apart?

Despite the success of *Speakerboxxx/The Love Below*, Patton and Benjamin have continually emphasized that they have no plans to split up and pursue solo careers. "We're not breaking up," Benjamin proclaimed around the time of the Grammy Awards, "but we're most definitely growing up." Patton reinforced that the duo's partnership was stronger than music. "He's just like my brother. I'm his kids' godfather—he's my kids' godfather. Our mamas hang out together."

Still, each has gotten involved in individual projects, leading to questions about their long-term plans. Patton likes to breed rare dogs like blue pit bull terriers, English bulldogs, Yorkshire terriers, and Neapolitan mastiffs. He owns Pitfall Kennels and has sold dogs to celebrities like tennis player Serena Williams and pop star Usher. He also runs the duo's OutKast Clothing Company and their Aquemini record label. In addition, he recently released a documentary about the band called *Big Boi's Boom Boom Room*.

——— *"* ———

"We're not breaking up,"
Benjamin proclaimed
around the time of the
2004 Grammy Awards,
"but we're most definitely
growing up." Patton
reinforced that the duo's
partnership was stronger
than music. "He's just like
my brother. I'm his kids'
godfather — he's my kids'
godfather. Our mamas
hang out together."

——— *"* ———

Benjamin enjoys painting pictures and selling them through the group's website. He also enjoys yoga and plans to start up his own line of retail clothing accessories, including ties, gloves, scarves, ascots, and bracelets. He has dabbled in acting, auditioning for the lead role in a proposed movie about Jimi Hendrix and appearing in a small role in *Hollywood Homicide* with Josh Hartnett and Harrison Ford. Benjamin has recently been filming *Be Cool*, the sequel to the hit film *Get Shorty*. In *Be Cool*, he plays a thug in a rap group called the Dub MDs. John Travolta, Uma Thurman, Cedric the Entertainer, Harvey Keitel, Danny DeVito, The Rock, and James Gandolfini are also appearing in the film. The costumes have become part of the fun for Benjamin. "I get to dress stupid over-the-top," he said. "Platinum jewelry, pants half-down my waist."

As the members of OutKast pursue their separate interests, they also seem to be diverging in their musical tastes as well, with Patton emphasizing rap and Benjamin moving toward a more eclectic mix. With so many individual projects and such different styles, many music critics and fans have wondered if OutKast will remain a group or if Patton and Benjamin will decide to go their separate ways.

MARRIAGE AND FAMILY

Benjamin is single, but in 1998 he and singer Erykah Badu had a son named Seven Sirius. The couple never married. Benjamin and Badu maintain an amicable relationship and share responsibility for Seven's upbringing, but he admits that he was initially hurt by their breakup. "When you've given love to someone and then take it away, that's terrible," he said. "I don't wanna do nobody else like that. When I was with Erykah, I wrote some terrible wraps." Benjamin also remains close to his mother, Sharon.

Patton is also unmarried, but he and his long-time girlfriend, Sherilita, have two sons: Bamboo, born in 2000, and Cross, born in 2001; he also has a daughter, Jordan, born in 1995, from an earlier relationship. Patton is a devoted father, but still insists that music will always be the most important thing in his life. "My work pays for their schools and everything else they need, so I gotta do it," he explained. "And I love performing. So why would I stop? My first love is music, then my kids. I ain't worried about much else."

SELECTED WORKS

Southernplayalisticadillacmuzik, 1994
ATLiens, 1996
Aquemini, 1998
Stankonia, 2000
Big Boi and Dré Present . . . OutKast, 2001
Speakerboxxx/The Love Below, 2003

HONORS AND AWARDS

Grammy Awards (National Academy of Recording Arts and Sciences): 2000 (two awards), Best Rap Album for *Stankonia*, Best Rap Performance by a Duo or Group for "Ms. Jackson"; 2002 (one award), Best Rap Performance by a Duo or Group for "The Whole World" featuring Killer Mike; 2003 (three awards), Album of the Year for *Speakerboxxx/The Love Below*, Best Rap Album for *Speakerboxxx/The Love Below*, Best Urban/Alternative Performance for "Hey Ya!"
Video Music Awards (MTV): 2001, Best Hip-Hop Video for "Ms. Jackson"
Image Awards (NAACP): 2004, Outstanding Duo or Group

FURTHER READING

Periodicals

Atlanta Journal-Constitution, Oct. 30, 2000, p.D1
Ebony, Jan. 2004, p.74
Jet, Feb. 2, 2004, p.58

Life, Nov. 3, 2000, p.E13
Los Angeles Sentinel, Nov. 11, 1998, p.8
Los Angeles Times, Dec. 22, 1996, p.78; Sep. 21, 2003, p.35
Newsweek, Oct. 30, 2000, p.88; Sep. 22, 2003, p.86
People, Feb. 16, 2004, p.87
Rolling Stone, Nov. 23, 2000, p.62; Nov. 13, 2003, p.62; Mar. 18, 2004, p.58
Time, Sep. 29, 2003, p.71; Feb. 16, 2004, p.87; Apr. 26, 2004, p.95

Online Articles

http://www.cbsnews.com/stories/2004/02/04/entertainment/main598016
.shtml
(*CBS News*, "OutKast Fans in for 'Weirdo' Ride," Feb. 4, 2004)
http://www.usatoday.com/life/music/news/2003-09-21-OutKast-main
_x.htm
(*USA Today*, "OutKast Has a Funky Formula," Sep. 21, 2003)
http://www.usatoday.com/life/music/news/2003-09-21-OutKast-albums
_x.htm
(*USA Today*, "Through the Years with OutKast," Sep. 22, 2003)

ADDRESS

OutKast
Arista Records/Zomba
137-139 West 25th Street
New York, NY 10001

WORLD WIDE WEB SITES

http://www.outkast.com
http://www.stankonia.com
http://www.aristarec.com/aristaweb/Outkast

Ronald Reagan 1911-2004

American Politician and Former Actor
40th President of the United States

BIRTH

Ronald Wilson Reagan was born on February 6, 1911, in Tampico, Illinois, to John Edward and Nelle Wilson Reagan. John was a shoe salesman and Nelle was a homemaker who also worked as a dressmaker. Ronald was the youngest of two boys in the family, with an older brother named Neil. When Ronald was born, his father said he looked like "a little bit of a fat Dutchman"; from then on, his nickname was "Dutch."

YOUTH

John Reagan was outgoing, ambitious — and an alcoholic. He often lost jobs, and the family moved from town to town in Illinois as he moved from job to job. Ronald Reagan remembered that the family didn't have a lot of money. "We were poor, but we didn't know we were poor," he recalled. Yet he didn't feel deprived and remembered his early life as "a rare Huck Finn idyll." He developed the sunny, optimistic disposition that he had throughout his life, first as an actor and later as a politician.

Still, his father's alcoholism affected the family deeply. Reagan recalled that once, when he was 11, he came home and found his father passed out on the front porch. He felt like just leaving his dad on the porch, stepping over him, and trying to forget the whole thing. But he thought better of that decision. "I bent over him, smelling the sharp odor of whiskey from the speakeasy. I got a fistful of his overcoat. Opening the door, I managed to drag him inside and get him to bed." He recalled in his autobiography that the incident proved to be "the first moment of accepting responsibility."

Reagan's mother, Nelle, was a hard-working, devout Christian, and she had a tremendous influence on Ronald. She shared her strong faith with her sons, who were raised in the Protestant faith in the Disciples of Christ Church. Ronald Reagan grew up at a time when alcoholism brought shame on the families of addicts. Yet Nelle Reagan had an enlightened and compassionate approach to the disease, and she taught her boys to love and forgive their father. "My mother told us — my brother and I when we were both just kids and she knew that we would be exposed to this and see it — that we must not turn against our father . . . that this was a sickness he could not help."

> **Reagan grew up at a time when alcoholism brought shame on the families of addicts. Yet his mother had an enlightened and compassionate approach to the disease, and she taught her boys to love and forgive their alcoholic father. "My mother told us — my brother and I when we were both just kids and she knew that we would be exposed to this and see it — that we must not turn against our father . . . that this was a sickness he could not help."**

LEFT: The Reagan
family Christmas
card, 1916 or 1917.

BELOW: Reagan
in the 1920s.

LEFT: Reagan as a lifeguard in
Lowell Park, Illinois, 1927

Nelle Reagan also loved the theater. With her encouragement, Ronald became involved in drama from a very young age, appearing in church pageants and later in high school theater. She also taught him to read when he was five, and Reagan spent many hours reading adventure stories by Edgar Rice Burroughs and other action writers. In addition, Nelle Reagan encouraged his optimistic, trusting nature and the belief that there was good to be found in every human being.

―――― **((** ――――

Reagan was among a group of students at his college who organized a strike to oppose plans to cut back faculty. Speaking to the group, "I discovered that an audience had a feel to it, and that the audience and I were together. When I came to actually presenting the motion ... there was no need for parliamentary procedure. They came to their feet with a roar. It was heady wine."

―――― **))** ――――

EDUCATION

Reagan went to school at the local public schools wherever his family lived. He had trouble reading as a young child and remembered that the blackboard was often a blur. Later, it was discovered that he was severely nearsighted, and after he got his first pair of glasses, he was able to see the board with ease. When Reagan was nine, the family settled in the Illinois town of Dixon. There, Ronald attended elementary and high school. At Northside High, he was a good student and an outstanding athlete, especially on the football field; he also appeared in school plays. After graduating from Northside in 1928, Reagan went on to Eureka College, a small, Christian school in Peoria, Illinois. He paid for his tuition partly through a scholarship and also by washing dishes and working as a lifeguard over the summers. He was an outstanding lifeguard and saved some 77 swimmers during his summers working at Dixon's Lowell Park.

Reagan studied economics at Eureka, but was more devoted to football and drama than to his studies. An average student in college, he was well-liked by his teachers and fellow students. His nearly photographic memory helped, too, whether he was reading a book just before a test or memorizing lines for a play. He had a chance to see live theater at Eureka and was especially moved by an antiwar play that came to town called *Journey's*

End. He identified with the idealistic young hero, and he yearned to act. "Nature was trying to tell me something," he said later, "namely that my heart is a ham loaf."

It was at Eureka that he got his first taste of politics, too. When the college president announced plans to cut back faculty, Reagan was among a group of students who organized a strike. Speaking to the group, "I discovered that an audience had a feel to it, and that the audience and I were together. When I came to actually presenting the motion . . . there was no need for parliamentary procedure. They came to their feet with a roar. It was heady wine." Reagan graduated from Eureka College in 1932.

FIRST JOBS

When Reagan left college in 1932, the country was in the grips of the Great Depression. During this era, which lasted for much of the 1930s, America and many other countries suffered a severe economic downturn. Millions of people had trouble finding jobs and providing food and shelter for their families. In fact, up to 25% of the population was out of work.

Yet despite the difficult economic times, within six weeks Reagan found a job he loved: he became a sports broadcaster with radio station WOC in Davenport, Iowa, covering the University of Iowa football games. Reagan was able to combine two things he knew and loved — football and acting. And acting came in handy in broadcasting in those days. When WOC was acquired by a larger station, WHO in Des Moines, Iowa, Reagan was hired by them to cover several sports on the radio, including the baseball games of the Chicago Cubs. In those pre-television times, the broadcaster relied on the information coming over the telegraph wire, then "created" the play-by-play. Reagan never saw the games he broadcast. Instead, he'd take the information from the tape off the wire, which just included the name of the batter and whether or not he'd made a hit. Reagan would review it quickly, then recreate the games for his audience, describing balls, strikes, hits, and outs, adding commentary, and embellishing whenever necessary.

Reagan recounted one memorable day when the telegraph transmission failed and he was on his own: "I had a ball on the way to the plate and there was no way to call it back. At the same time, I was convinced that a ball game tied up in the ninth inning was no time to tell my audience we had lost contact with the game." He went on to describe a series of foul balls that went on for quite some time, until the transmission was repaired and he could continue with what was going on in the "real" game. The audience never knew the difference. The anecdote became one of Reagan's favorite stories to tell about his radio days.

ABOVE: Reagan as an announcer for WHO radio in Des Moines, Iowa, 1934-1937.

ABOVE: A still of Reagan from the film Knute Rockne — All American, *1940.*

RIGHT: Reagan in the U.S. Army Air Force, 1940s.

CAREER IN HOLLYWOOD

What Reagan wanted most in those days was to be an actor, so on a 1937 trip to California to cover the Cubs for WHO he took a screen test in Hollywood. Much to his delight, he was hired by Warner Brothers at $200 a week, a great salary in those tough times. Reagan embarked on a film career that included 53 movies, including his first, *Love Is in the Air,* in which he played a radio announcer. He was never an A-list actor, but his handsome, athletic, and friendly presence made him a popular one.

In 1940, while filming *Brother Rat,* he met Jane Wyman, who became his first wife. That same year he lobbied for, and won, the role that made him famous. He played football player George Gipp in a film about Knute Rockne, Notre Dame's legendary football coach. In *Knute Rockne — All American,* Reagan appeared in the film's most famous scene, where Gipp, on his deathbed, pleads with Rockne to "win one for the Gipper." Years later, Reagan said that he still "got a lump in my throat . . . just thinking about it." The role became identified with him throughout his career, and, like "Dutch," "Gipper" became a nickname.

In 1942 Reagan appeared in *King's Row,* which is considered his best film. He plays a womanizer named Drake McHugh, who seduces the daughter of a surgeon in a small town. In revenge, the sadistic doctor amputates Drake's legs. Waking up, Reagan's character screams, "Where's the rest of me?" The line became as closely associated with Reagan as his famous Gipper phrase, and also provided him with the title of his autobiography, which was published in 1965.

King's Row was well-received, and Reagan's performance was widely praised, but it was his last Hollywood film for a few years. It appeared just as the U.S. entered World War II, and Reagan tried to enlist. His eyesight was so poor that he wasn't considered fit for combat, so he spent the war stateside, making training films for the U.S. armed services. After the war, Reagan continued to act in many films, most of them forgettable. He starred in a series as Brass Bancroft, Secret Service Agent, and also co-starred with a chimp named Bonzo in several films.

Screen Actors Guild

But by then, Reagan's interests had changed. In 1941, he had been appointed to the board of the Screen Actors Guild (SAG), the union representing movie actors. He became more and more involved in his work with the Guild, and was elected president of SAG five times. In 1946 Reagan was asked to mediate a dispute that brought him into contact with some union leaders who were allegedly Communists. This happened in the era after World War II, when the American political landscape was transformed by changes in world politics. During the Depression of the 1930s, some Americans, including actors, had been drawn to Communism as a possible way out of the financial and social misery of the times. After World War II, the U.S. and the Communist Soviet Union emerged as the two superpowers in the world. These two nations became locked in the conflict known as the Cold War — a war defined not by open warfare, but by escalating hostilities between the two nations, one democratic and one Communist, and the division of the major world governments into pro-U.S. and pro-Soviet nations. The era was also defined by mutual distrust, suspicion, hostility, and the constant underlying fear of a third world war that might destroy humanity.

> *Reagan met the actress Nancy Davis in Hollywood; they married in 1952. He called Nancy the most important thing in his life. "Put simply, my life really began when I met her and has been rich and full ever since," he said.*

The tensions created by the Cold War had a tremendous influence on the political climate in the U.S. In the U.S. House of Representatives, the House Un-American Activities Committee, or HUAC, was searching to root out and expose Communists in every industry, including the movie industry. In doing so, they sometimes ruined the lives and careers of innocent people. Simply to be accused, or "named," before the committee was often enough to get an individual "blacklisted" — which took away their ability to make a living and ruined their reputations. As a labor leader, Reagan was called to testify before HUAC in 1947. When asked to "name names" of Communists in the film industry, Reagan refused. Years later, historian Garry Wills uncovered evidence, including some in released FBI files, that Reagan had indeed given the government names, in secret.

Reagan's growing interest in politics had a damaging effect on his marriage to Jane Wyman. She filed for divorce in 1948, alleging "mental cruelty." Reagan was devastated by the divorce and considered it the darkest time of his life. A few years later, he met the actress Nancy Davis in Hollywood; they married in 1952. They were a devoted couple, and Reagan called Nancy the most important thing in his life. "Put simply, my life really began when I met her and has been rich and full ever since," he said.

A Change of Political Philosophy

Around this time, Reagan began to have a change of heart politically. He had been a lifelong Democrat, believing in the New Deal concepts developed during the presidency of Franklin Delano Roosevelt (1933-1945). As president during much of the Depression, Roosevelt had created the New Deal, which promoted a strong federal government and domestic programs designed to help struggling Americans financially. Reagan described himself at the time as a "near-hopeless hemophiliac liberal." But while continuing to support Democratic candidates, he also began to be drawn to the Republican Party. He even headed a movement called Democrats for Dwight Eisenhower when Ike ran for President in 1952 and 1956.

Reagan and "General Electric Theater," 1954-1962.

Reagan's philosophy was changing at the same time his career took a turn, from film to television. Soon he was hired by General Electric for a new series, "General Electric Theater," one of the first theatrical series on TV. Every week, Reagan appeared in millions of homes all over the country as host and sometimes as star of the television drama series. As part of his contract, he also appeared at GE plants throughout the country, giving speeches to the employees. Thus, he had a forum to introduce himself to Americans throughout the nation and to speak with them one-on-one. What he learned there changed him forever.

Between 1954 and 1962, Reagan visited 139 GE plants, meeting some 250,000 employees, and, he recalled, "enjoying every whizzing minute of it." In his countless speeches, he honed his delivery and listened to the concerns of the American public. "That did much to shape my ideas," he said. "These employees I was meeting were a cross section of Americans, and damn it, too many of our political leaders, our labor leaders, and certainly a lot of geniuses on Madison Avenue, have underestimated them. They want the truth, they are friendly and helpful, intelligent and alert. They are concerned with their very firm personal liberties. And they are moral." What he heard made Reagan reconsider his politics and his career.

In 1960, Reagan campaigned for Republican presidential candidate Richard Nixon as a "Democrat for Nixon," and in 1962 he officially switched his political affiliation from Democrat to Republican. That same year, the political rhetoric of his speeches had grown so conservative that GE let him go. He used key phrases like "Government is not the solution to our problem. Government is the problem," and attacked large government subsidized programs, like Social Security and the Tennessee Valley Authority (TVA). The TVA is a federally funded program created in the 1930s to prevent flooding and to develop the energy resources of the Tennessee River Valley. By the 1960s, GE had millions of dollars in contracts with the TVA to provide electricity to the area, so Reagan's criticisms directly conflicted with the company's business.

―――― " ――――

In 1964, Reagan gave a speech that mesmerized conservative Republicans and set his course in politics. "You and I have a rendezvous with destiny," he said. "We will preserve for our children this, the last best hope of man on earth, or we will sentence them to take the first step into a thousand years of darkness."

―――― " ――――

A Major Speech

In 1964, Reagan gave a speech, "A Time for Choosing," that mesmerized conservative Republicans and set his course in politics. Reagan spoke as part of a nationally televised broadcast in support of Barry Goldwater, the arch-conservative Republican presidential candidate that year. He attacked the "Great Society" programs of then-President Lyndon Johnson, claiming they were the type of "big government" that, according to Reagan, compromised the future of the nation. "You and I have a rendezvous with destiny," he told them. "We will preserve for our children this, the last best hope of man on earth, or we will sentence them to take the first step into a thousand years of darkness."

Goldwater went down to defeat in one of the biggest landslides in history, but Ronald Reagan had made a name for himself in politics.

CAREER IN POLITICS

In a political career that spanned more than 30 years, Ronald Reagan symbolized the conservative movement in American politics. From his surprise election as governor of California to his election as President of the United States, he confounded critics and pundits alike. He appealed directly to voters with his positive, optimistic message of America as a place of endless possibilities, combined with his promise to "get government off the backs" of the American people.

Campaigning as candidate for governor of California, November 1966.

That potential was first seen by a group of California businessman, who contacted Reagan soon after the 1964 presidential election. This wealthy group of conservative Republicans would promote and finance Reagan throughout his political career. In 1964, they wanted Reagan to run for governor of California, and they proceeded to form his campaign. Reagan announced his candidacy in January 1966, taking on a popular Democratic governor, Pat Brown. Like many of Reagan's political opponents, Brown didn't take Reagan seriously, making light of his Hollywood career. But Reagan was serious and ran on a platform that promised to reduce the size of government and "clean up the mess at Berkeley," referring to the student protests that had begun to foment at the University of California at Berkeley and at college campuses all around the nation.

Governor of California

Reagan surprised many when he beat Brown by over one million votes to win the race for governor in 1966. He then served two terms as governor, from 1966 to 1974. As governor, he gained a reputation as a pragmatic, effective leader who could forge compromises between parties and run a state with one of the largest economies in the world. According to Lou Cannon, a journalist who followed Reagan from California to Washington and wrote an acclaimed biography of him, the secret to Reagan's success wasn't easy to explain. "On one level, he seemed the 'citizen-politician' he claimed to be, almost completely ignorant of even civics-books information about how bills were passed or how an administration functioned. But on another level, he seemed the most consummate and effective

Governor-elect Reagan and Governor Edmund G. Brown meet after Reagan's landslide victory over Brown, November 1966.

politician I had ever met." It was that political savvy that took him to the top of American politics.

Although Reagan had campaigned on a platform that included cutting taxes and spending, as governor he inherited a large budget deficit and a Democratic state legislature. As would happen throughout his political career, he agreed to increase taxes; by the time his second term was over, the state's budget had doubled. Reagan also signed legislation in welfare, education, and tax reform. But by the end of his years of governor in 1974, he had his eyes on a bigger prize: the presidency.

Running for President

Reagan had actually made his interest in the office known in 1968, when Richard Nixon was the presumptive candidate for the Republicans. The movement to draft Reagan as the Republican candidate in 1968 was begun by political adviser Lyn Nofziger and backed by the wealthy California businessmen who had encouraged Reagan to run for governor. He ran in the early primaries and stayed in the race until the Republican convention, when he gave his support to Nixon. Nixon beat Democrat Hubert Humphrey to win the election in 1968 and was reelected in 1972, but resigned from office in the wake of the Watergate scandal.

The term Watergate refers to a political scandal that occurred from 1972-1974 during Nixon's presidency. A group of people linked to his re-election campaign were arrested while committing a burglary at the offices of the Democratic Party headquarters at the Watergate Hotel in Washington, D.C. After their arrests, Nixon and his aides created a massive cover-up to conceal any links between the burglars and the White House. But their efforts were unsuccessful, as journalists and other investigators soon revealed the involvement of the President and his aides. Americans became angry and disillusioned as they learned about Watergate, and Nixon became the first president in U.S. history to resign from office. (For more information on Richard Nixon, see *Biography Today*, Sept. 1994.)

Reagan had been a great supporter of Nixon throughout the turmoil of Watergate, and he was deeply disappointed to learn that Nixon had lied to the American people. By the time of Nixon's resignation, Reagan was once again a private citizen. He began to write a newspaper column, and he also broadcast a weekly commentary on 200 radio stations nationwide. He went back to the "mashed potato circuit" — his term for the type of speaking engagements he'd done for GE — which brought him in touch with many potential voters. Even out of elected office, Reagan reached out to millions of Americans every week, promoting his message of conservative, Republican government. In doing this, he solidified his voting base in a way that confounded the general wisdom among politicians. He used the appeal he'd enjoyed as an actor to continue to attract interest as a potential political candidate. As Lou Cannon writes in his biography, "the earnest, affable Reagan was rapidly forming a relationship with potential voters that was an extension of the bond he had forged with movie and television audiences during his long career. . . .He was the wholesome citizen-hero who inhabits our democratic imaginations, an Everyman who was slow to anger but willing to fight for the right."

> **"**
>
> *"The earnest, affable Reagan was rapidly forming a relationship with potential voters that was an extension of the bond he had forged with movie and television audiences during his long career. . . . He was the wholesome citizen-hero who inhabits our democratic imaginations, an Everyman who was slow to anger but willing to fight for the right."*
> *— Lou Cannon, Reagan biographer*
>
> **"**

In 1976, Reagan again made a run for the Republican nomination for president, going head-to-head with President Gerald Ford in the Republican primaries. He almost beat Ford, an incumbent president, missing the nomination at that year's convention by a vote of 1,187 to 1,070. That fall, Ford ran against Democrat Jimmy Carter, who narrowly won the presidency. Reagan regrouped, planning to launch his challenge to Carter in 1980.

> *In accepting the Republican nomination at the 1980 convention, Reagan outlined the political philosophy that would prove a winning one: "They say that the United States has had its day in the sun, that our nation has passed its zenith. They expect you to tell your children that the American people no longer have the will to cope with their problems, that the future will be one of sacrifice and few opportunities. My fellow citizens, I utterly reject that view."*

The Election of 1980

Reagan announced his candidacy for the Republican nomination in 1980 and ran well in the primaries. His principal opposition was George H.W. Bush, whom he chose as his vice presidential running mate. In accepting the Republican nomination at the convention that year, Reagan outlined the political philosophy that would prove a winning one: "They say that the United States has had its day in the sun, that our nation has passed its zenith. They expect you to tell your children that the American people no longer have the will to cope with their problems, that the future will be one of sacrifice and few opportunities. My fellow citizens, I utterly reject that view."

Jimmy Carter's term as president had been troubled. Domestically, high inflation, high interest rates, and high unemployment made the economy stagnant. On the international front, the U.S. was facing down the Soviet Union, which had invaded Afghanistan. More urgently, the government of the Shah of Iran had been toppled by an Islamic fundamentalist movement; in November 1979, Iranian militants stormed the U.S. embassy in Tehran and took 52 Americans hostage. Throughout their long ordeal, their fate became an obsession with the American public and the media; the ABC-TV show "Nightline" was begun in 1979 specifically to monitor the situation.

Reagan campaigning for president in November 1980 in Peoria, Illinois, with former President Gerald Ford and Reagan's running mate George H. W. Bush.

Despite all his troubles, Carter underestimated his Republican opponent's appeal to American voters. He called Reagan "dangerous," but that didn't affect Reagan's standing in the polls. When the Democrats made an issue of Reagan's age—he was 69 years old when he was running—he showed, through his vigor on the campaign trail and his robust good health, that he was equal to the task. In televised debates, Carter tried to attack Reagan's record on issues like Medicare, but Reagan countered with lines like, "There you go again," diminishing Carter's effectiveness. One line in particular resonated with voters: Reagan asked the American public, "Are you better off today than you were four years ago?" He ran on a platform that promised a 30% tax cut, reductions in government spending, and a balanced budget. He questioned Carter's defense policy against the Soviet Union and the threat of Communism around the world. And he told the American people that its best days were ahead, offering his optimistic vision of the country in difficult times.

President of the United States

On November 4, 1980, Reagan was elected President of the United States in an overwhelming victory. He won 50.7% of the vote to Carter's 41% (an additional 6.6% of voters cast their ballots for independent candidate John Anderson). Reagan was later reelected in a landslide to a second term in office, serving as president from 1981 until 1989.

The Reagans celebrating in the limousine in the inaugural parade, January 1981.

Reagan's first term in office got off to a good start: on the day of his inauguration, January 20, 1981, the government of Iran released the 52 American hostages, who had been held for 444 days. As President, Reagan set out his policies immediately. He called for tax cuts and cuts in government spending, especially in welfare programs, but argued for large defense budgets. At the same time, he brought a very different approach to the position of President. Reagan believed in balancing work and free time. He delegated responsibility to staff, worked a regular eight-hour day, and enjoyed taking naps. He spent a good deal of time away from Washington, at his beloved California ranch.

As President, Reagan again showed the same lack of interest in and knowledge of the everyday responsibilities of governing that he had exhibited as governor of California. In his biography, Lou Cannon relates how Reagan's staff prepared a daily list of meetings and appointments for him, along with 3 x 5 cards outlining his positions on political issues. Once, in a meeting with then-Speaker of the House Tip O'Neill, the congressman became furious with the President, who refused to talk to the Speaker directly, referring instead to the points on the 3 x 5 cards. But Reagan was able to talk about some issues in detail and with a great deal of authority. And he never lost his ability to talk directly to the American people and to move them. For this, he gained the title he was known for in the presidency, "The Great Communicator."

Shortly after taking office, Reagan endured a terrible ordeal: an assassination attempt. On March 30, 1981, Reagan and three others were shot by John Hinckley, Jr., outside a Washington hotel. The President was wounded in the lung; his press secretary, James Brady, was struck in the head by a bullet. When Reagan was rushed to the hospital, his sense of humor remained intact. While being wheeled into surgery, he said to the doctors, "Please tell me you're Republicans." When he first spoke with Nancy Reagan, he told her, "Honey, I forgot to duck." In recovery he joked, "If I had had this much attention in Hollywood, I would have stayed." After the shooting, James Brady suffered permanent brain damage and was partially paralyzed for life. He and his wife, Sarah Brady, became active supporters of gun control. Their work resulted in the Brady Bill, legislation that mandated a waiting period before people could buy handguns and created a system for national criminal background checks for prospective gun buyers.

——— **"** ———

"Ronald Reagan's domestic policies . . . were almost uniformly appalling. He shifted the tax burden downward, exacerbated economic inequality, created gigantic deficits, undermined environmental, civil-rights, and labor protections, neglected the AIDS epidemic, and packed the courts with reactionary mediocrities. . . . Reagan was a pretty poor President in a lot of way."
— Edmund Morris, Reagan biographer

——— **"** ———

Domestic Issues

Back at work, Reagan and his aides lobbied hard for his tax cut package, and he got most of what he wanted: a 25% reduction in taxes and $35 billion trimmed from the federal budget, but with additional spending for defense. The Federal Reserve Board raised interest rates (the rate that banks charge customers to lend them money) to try to stem inflation, and the immediate result was a recession, with unemployment rising to over 10%, and the poverty rate growing at a rapid clip. Many of the tax cuts targeted social services programs that were designed to help poor people, including health care, food assistance, welfare, and school lunch programs, which further contributed to the difficulties faced by the poor.

Reagan at work in the Oval Office.

Reagan's economic policy, called "Reaganomics," was based on an economic theory known as "supply-side economics," which argues that tax cuts promote economic growth. This premise, which is also known as "trickle-down economics," says that if wealthy individuals and businesses get a tax break, they would put money back into the economy in the form of consumer spending and investment in businesses. Stimulating savings and investments, therefore, would create higher productivity, jobs, and profits.

Reagan firmly believed that things would get better, and gradually, they did. In the eight years of his presidency, the prime interest rate fell from 15.3% to 9.3%; inflation fell from 12.5% to 4.4%; and unemployment fell from 10.8% to 5.5%. Whether or not the positive economic news was due to Reagan's policies—or other factors—is still debated by economists. Some experts note that the rise in poverty levels during his administration demonstrated his lack of concern for the poor and his insistence on high spending for defense led to a huge national deficit. Still, the turnaround in the economy is considered one of the highlights of the Reagan presidency.

International Issues

Reagan had been a fervent anti-Communist since his days in Hollywood. As President, he saw it as his mission to try to destroy Communism and its grip on millions the world over. In a speech early in his presidency, he referred to the Soviet Union as "the Evil Empire," and he vowed to do all he could to end Communism. He made speeches outlining the U.S. defensive strategy against the Soviet Union and proposed a controversial defense system called the Space Defense Initiative (SDI). The SDI would create a "shield" in space to protect the U.S. from a Soviet nuclear attack; it was also called "Star Wars" since it would destroy missiles from space. Many believed the plan was not tenable, but it had an immediate effect. It forced the Soviet Union to retaliate by spending furiously on its military, escalating the arms race between the nations and weakening an already fragile Soviet economy.

At the same time, a new leader came to head the Soviet Union, Premier Mikhail Gorbachev. Gorbachev was not a typical hard-liner. Instead, he was a reformer, offering new options, called *glasnost* (openness) and *perestroika* (reform), Russian terms for an opening up of ideas and encouraging change from within the Soviet Union. He and Reagan had a series of historic meetings that were first hostile, then gradually more cordial, as the conservative Republican and the Communist leader became friends. In the course of their relationship, Reagan went from a famous speech before the Berlin Wall in which he charged the Soviet leader, "Mr. Gorbachev, tear down this wall," to signing historic treaties to destroy the nuclear arsenals of both nations. And just one year after Reagan left office, in 1989, the Berlin Wall—the symbol of Soviet domination throughout the world—did

———— *"* ————

"Clare Booth Luce famously said that each President is remembered for a sentence: 'He freed the slaves'; 'He made the Louisiana Purchase.'... Ronald Reagan knew going in the sentence he wanted, and he got it. He guided the American victory in the Cold War. Under his leadership, a conflict that had absorbed a half-century of Western blood and treasure was ended—and the good guys finally won."
— Peggy Noonan, former speechwriter for President Reagan

———— *"* ————

Reagan with Vice President George H. W. Bush and Soviet President Mikhail Gorbachev on Governor's Island, New York.

come tumbling down, as Communist nations throughout Eastern Europe broke free from Soviet control and established democracies. Then, in December 1991, the Soviet Union itself collapsed, ending more than 70 years of Communist rule. In the opinion of many, it was Reagan's determination to force the Soviet Union to spend so much on defense that caused the demise of Communism and the end of the Cold War. Many consider Reagan's fight against Communism to be the greatest achievement of his presidency.

During his presidency, Reagan also dealt with terrorist threats from abroad. In 1983, a suicide bomber destroyed the barracks housing a U.S. Marines peacekeeping force in Lebanon, killing 241 American troops. Reagan took personal responsibility for the incident and removed all U.S. troops from the area within months. In 1986, there was a terrorist bombing at a nightclub in Berlin, which killed a U.S. serviceman. In retaliation, Reagan sent bombers to Libya, home of Muammar Qaddafi, a known sponsor of terrorists.

The Iran-Contra Affair

Perhaps the most controversial episode in Reagan's presidency was the Iran-Contra affair. In the mid-1980s terrorists were holding seven American hostages in Lebanon, and Reagan's efforts to free them led to the greatest crisis in his administration. It began in 1985. Iran and Iraq were at war, and Iran made a secret request to buy weapons from the U.S. Several members of the administration, notably National Security Adviser Robert McFarlane, John Poindexter, and Lt. Colonel Oliver North, together conspired to sell arms to Iran. At that time, Iran was an enemy of the U.S. and was also an ally of the Shiite terrorists who were holding the American hostages. In exchange for the weapons, Iran was to negotiate the return of the hostages. Selling arms to Iran violated two of Reagan's stated principles: he opposed negotiating for hostages and he opposed aiding Iran.

Further, McFarlane, Poindexter, and North had taken the money from the sales of arms to Iran and sent the money to Nicaragua to fund the group known as the Contras. The anti-Communist Contras were fighting the pro-Communist Sandinistas for control of the country. Reagan had made clear his support for the Contras; but what was less clear was whether he ever gave Poindexter, North, and McFarlane the authorization for what was clearly an illegal activity. It was a violation of the Boland Amendment, a congressional act that forbid any U.S. military aid to the Contras.

The allegations first came to light in a Lebanese newspaper. Initially Reagan vehemently denied it, then a week later he went on television and retracted his earlier denial. The U.S. Congress held an investigation, after which North was fired and Poindexter resigned. McFarlane pled guilty to withholding information from Congress. But most damaging to Reagan was that when he testified, it was clear that he was not in control of his administration. When asked whether he gave his approval to the initial idea of arms-for-hostages, Reagan said he couldn't remember. It was unclear exactly what had happened. Was Reagan aware of the illegal activities, had he approved them, and was he now lying to the American public? Or was he simply unaware of what was going on in his own administration? Either way, it was disturbing to Americans and damaging to Reagan's reputation.

Yet despite Iran-Contra, Reagan did not seem to suffer in the eyes of the public for long. When he left office, his approval ratings remained high. He was, as Congresswoman Patricia Schroeder had so aptly called him, the "Teflon President." It was hard to make anything negative stick to him.

Leaving the White House

Reagan left the White House in January 1989 and headed home to California and his beloved ranch. He had loved being President, but he was ready to retire and enjoy life as a private citizen again. He spent time on the ranch riding his horse and clearing brush. At the end of 1989, he had a

———— " ————

In 1994, Ronald Reagan wrote a letter to the American people revealing that he had been diagnosed with Alzheimer's disease. "Let me thank you, the American people, for giving me the great honor of allowing me to serve as your President. When the Lord calls me home, whenever that may be, I will leave with the greatest love for this country of ours and eternal optimism for its future. I now begin the journey that will lead me into the sunset of my life. I know that for America there will always be a bright dawn ahead."

———— " ————

serious fall while riding that injured his head and required surgery. After that, he had to give up riding. He continued to travel and give speeches, but by the early 1990s, he began to show signs of mental deterioration. At the Republican Convention in 1992, he seemed tired and confused, unlike the "Great Communicator" and leader of the past. At other public events he seemed disoriented and unsure of himself.

In 1994, Ronald Reagan wrote a letter to the American people revealing that he had been diagnosed with Alzheimer's disease. The disease causes irreversible damage to the brain, ending in dementia and death. There is no cure. With characteristic humility and warmth, Reagan wrote: "Let me thank you, the American people, for giving me the great honor of allowing me to serve as your President. When the Lord calls me home, whenever that may be, I will leave with the greatest love for this country of ours and eternal optimism for its future. I now begin the journey that will lead me into the sunset of my life. I know that for America there will always be a bright dawn ahead."

The Reagans had decided to make the diagnosis public to help raise awareness of the disease and also to shed light on its effects on family members. In the past decade, much has been learned about Alzheimer's, including some of its genetic components; it is now believed to be a hereditary disease. In Reagan's case, both his mother and brother suffered from the disease. After his announcement, Reagan continued to go to his office for a while and to play golf. But in later years he was not able to leave the house in Bel-Air, California, where he and Nancy Reagan lived.

On June 5, 2004, Ronald Reagan died at the age of 93. There was an immediate outpouring of grief from the nation, and Reagan was given a full

The President and First Lady about to enter the helicopter as they leave Washington on his last day in office, January 1989.

state funeral in Washington, D.C. There, thousands of Americans came to view his casket and to pay their last respects. His funeral service was broadcast around the world and attended by current President George W. Bush, as well as all the living past Presidents—Gerald Ford, Jimmy Carter, George H.W. Bush, and Bill Clinton. In addition, hundreds of world leaders attended the funeral, past and present, including his good friend and former British Prime Minister Margaret Thatcher and former Soviet leader Mikhail Gorbachev. Now weakened by a series of strokes, Thatcher gave a warm video tribute to her former colleague and Cold Warrior. Reagan was buried at his presidential library in Simi Valley, California.

LEGACY

Reagan's legacy lies in his achievements in both domestic and foreign policy. And yet that legacy is mixed. His economic policies turned around a financial crisis fueled by inflation, high interest rates, and high unemployment, yet the deficit also increased enormously. While he imagined America as "a shining city on a hill," there were some who saw it differently. As Mario Cuomo said in his address to the Democratic Convention in 1984, "The hard truth is that not everyone is sharing in this city's splendor and glory. . . . There's another part to the shining city; the part where some people can't pay their mortgages and most young people can't afford one, where students can't afford the education they need and middle-class parents watch the dreams they hold for their children evaporate."

——— *"* ———

In the words of historian Kenneth Lynn, "Reagan fulfilled a restorative function we desperately needed. His belief that we can come out of our travail with a renewed strength, his ebullience, his optimism, and his lack of guilt in his personal life and in America in general were a breath of fresh air. To have someone speak in terms of possibility, of limitlessness rather than of limits, was an elixir."

——— *"* ———

In foreign policy, Reagan's legacy, despite Iran-Contra, rests on the part he played in ending the Cold War and on his stance against the Soviet Union and Communism. According to presidential historian Michael Beschloss, he was indispensable. "His first-term efforts to escalate the competition with the Soviet Union and his revival of American willpower may well have helped to usher in the reformist Gorbachev. . . . Reagan's defense of SDI, so ridiculed at the time, pressed Gorbachev, while his economy was collapsing, to make arms deals and improve relations with the West, which contributed to the unraveling of his empire. After FDR's death in 1945, the *New York Times* predicted that 'men will thank God on their knees 100 years from now' that FDR had been the president to fight Hitler and Tojo. It is not too much to suggest that, with Ronald Reagan's death, Americans might now give similar thanks that they twice elected a president who saw the chance to end the Cold War in his own time."

But perhaps Reagan is best remembered for his confidence, hopefulness, and optimism, an optimism "so radiant that it seemed almost a force of

*A Reagan family photo: (standing, from left to right) Geoffrey Davis,
Dennis Revell, Michael Reagan, Cameron Reagan, President Reagan, Neil Reagan,
Dr. Richard Davis, Ron Reagan; (sitting, from left to right) Anne Davis,
Maureen Reagan, Colleen Reagan, Nancy Reagan, Bess Reagan,
Patricia Davis, Patti Davis, Doria Reagan.*

nature," according to the *New York Times*. He came to the presidency at a
time when many Americans needed to be reassured that the nation was
still proud and strong. In the words of historian Kenneth Lynn, "Reagan
fulfilled a restorative function we desperately needed. His belief that we
can come out of our travail with a renewed strength, his ebullience, his
optimism, and his lack of guilt in his personal life and in America in general were a breath of fresh air. To have someone speak in terms of possibility, of limitlessness rather than of limits, was an elixir."

MARRIAGE AND FAMILY

Reagan was married twice. He married actress Jane Wyman in 1940, and
they had two children: Maureen, born in 1941, and Michael, whom they
adopted in 1945. Wyman filed for divorce in 1948. Neither Reagan nor Wyman ever publicly discussed the divorce. In 1952, he married Nancy Davis,

who was also an actress when they met. They had two children: Patricia, born in 1952, and Ronald, born in 1958. Ronald and Nancy Reagan spent many of their happiest times at their California ranch, Rancho del Cielo.

WRITINGS

Where's the Rest of Me? 1965
An American Life, 1990

FURTHER READING

Books

Buckley, William F. *Ronald Reagan: An American Hero*, 2001
Cannon, Lou. *President Reagan: The Role of a Lifetime*, 1991; rev. ed., 2000
Encyclopedia Britannica, 2004
Morris, Edmund. *Dutch: A Memoir of Ronald Reagan*, 1999
Reagan, Ronald. *Where's the Rest of Me?* 1965
Reagan, Ronald. *An American Life*, 1990
World Book Encyclopedia, 2004

Periodicals

Current Biography Yearbook, 1949, 1967, 1982
Los Angeles Times, June 6, 2004, p.A1, A31, A34, A42; June 7, p.A1, A9, A11, E1, E2, E3
New York Times, June 6, 2004, p.A1; June 7, 2004, p.A28 and A29; June 8, 2004, p.A23; June 11, 2004, p.A1; June 12, 2004, p.A1; June 15, 2004, p.D5
New Yorker, June 28, 2004, p.69
Newsweek, Special Commemorative Edition, June 14, 2004
Time, Special Commemorative Issue, June 14, 2004
Times (London), June 7, 2004, Features, p.28
Wall Street Journal, June 7, 2004, p.A1; June 8, 2004, p.A16 and A17
Washington Post, June 6, 2004, p.A1, p.A8

WORLD WIDE WEB SITES

http://www.ipl.org/POTUS
http://www.reaganlibrary.com
http://www.pbs.org/wgbh/amex/reagan/timeline/index.html
http://www.whitehouse.gov

Ricardo Sanchez 1951-

American Lieutenant General, United States Army
Former Commanding General of U.S. and Coalition
Forces in Iraq

BIRTH

Ricardo Sanchez was born in 1951 in Rio Grande City, Texas.
His father, Domingo Sanchez, was a welder for a gravel company. His mother, Maria Elena Sauceda, worked at a variety of
jobs. Ricardo was the second child born to his parents: he has
three brothers and two sisters, as well as two half brothers.

YOUTH

Rio Grande City is in the far southern part of Texas and takes its name from the river that flows past the town and forms the border between the United States and Mexico. As he grew up, Ricardo was able to look across the Rio Grande and see the country where his ancestors had lived. His father and mother had spent their lives on the Texas side of the border, but both of their families originally hailed from Mexico.

In a lot of ways, southern Texas is not much different from Mexico. The weather is hot and dry, and many of the residents speak Spanish more than English. It's also a poor area where lots of people struggle to get by. Starr County, where Rio Grande City is located, was named the poorest county in the United States in the 2000 Census, and it didn't fare much better in the years when Ricardo was growing up.

Sanchez has described his background as "dirt poor." For several years the family lived in a one-room house on the outskirts of Rio Grande City. There was no indoor plumbing, so they had to use an outdoor bathroom (an outhouse) and get their water from a faucet in the yard. At that point the family included Ricardo, his parents, and two siblings, who all shared the tiny home. Because there were no bedrooms, they used a metal table to separate the area where they slept from the area where they ate their meals. Later, the family moved to a better house with two bedrooms, a kitchen, and a living room, but they still didn't have an indoor toilet.

> *"[We] really looked forward to Thursdays, every other week as I recall, because that was when Mom would go to the VA relief center to draw our rations. . . . That meant we would have some meat, cheese, and butter in the house for at least a couple of days. With a family of six, that didn't last long, and there were many days when we had only beans and rice."*

Learning from His Mom

To make matters worse, Sanchez's parents divorced when he was nine years old. The children stayed with their mother, who faced the tough job of supporting her large family. Maria Elena worked a full-time job, and she also got some help from welfare programs. Sanchez said that "we really looked forward to Thursdays, every other week as I recall, because that was when

Mom would go to the VA [Veteran's Administration] relief center to draw our rations. . . . That meant we would have some meat, cheese, and butter in the house for at least a couple of days. With a family of six, that didn't last long, and there were many days when we had only beans and rice."

Even though times were tough, Sanchez recalls many good things about his childhood. "We weren't suffering," he once said. "We never went hungry that I could remember. It was very basic living, a good environment for family values. It taught you a lot of discipline." A lot of the lessons came directly from his mother, and the biggest one was the importance of education. Maria Elena had dropped out of school at a young age. As an adult, she wanted a second chance at completing her studies, so she managed to attend night classes even though she was busy with work and raising her family. Eventually she earned her general equivalency degree (GED). Sanchez has said that it was his mother's "unbelievable desire to succeed in getting her GED, in spite of all obstacles, that taught me perseverance, dedication, focus and, of course, the will to succeed."

——— **"** ———

"We weren't suffering," Sanchez once said. "We never went hungry that I could remember. It was very basic living, a good environment for family values. It taught you a lot of discipline."

——— **"** ———

While still very young, Sanchez showed that he was ready to imitate his mom's hard work. He had his first job at age six. Over the years he worked in his uncle's tailor shop, swept the floor at a drug store, and delivered clothes for a dry cleaner. But, like his mom, he would put his biggest effort into his studies.

"At the time, you don't look at it as being tough," Sanchez recalled about those early days. "It's just the condition that you exist in. In reality, when you look back, there were some pretty tough times. But our mother was very focused on making sure we got our education, and she was a pretty good disciplinarian, too, making sure that we were not messing around and getting into trouble and making sure that we were at school. When we thought otherwise, she had her means of getting us back in line."

EDUCATION

Maria Elena put a lot of emphasis on her children's schooling. "I told them that I wanted them to have the education that my parents didn't give me," she recalled. Sanchez got along okay in his first years of schooling, but when he was in the sixth grade, he faced a new challenge. When he had difficulty solving a math problem in class, his teacher called him a "dummy." It could have been a discouraging incident, but Sanchez turned it to his advantage. "I was going to show her that I was better than that," he recalled, and he applied himself to his math studies like never before. Soon, math was his favorite subject, and he would later major in the subject in college. "That negative event had a tremendous impact on my life," Sanchez said of the teacher's comment. "It really made me who I am today. . . . It was the first instance where I remember being challenged and reacting in a way that was very focused in order to prove people wrong."

Still, like many other kids Sanchez grew tired of classes. When he was 13, he and his older brother announced that they didn't want to go to school anymore. Rather than argue with them, their mother told them that they could give up school only if they went to work picking cotton. The boys agreed, and the next morning they went to work in the fields at five a.m. "They came home and they were very tired," Maria Elena told the *Corpus Christi Caller-Times*, "but I just gave them some dinner and told them, 'Go to bed because tomorrow you have to wake up early. You have to get up at 5 a.m. and pick cotton for the rest of your life.'" Sanchez and his brother decided that school was easier than the fields, and they went back to hitting the books.

> *"At the time, you don't look at it as being tough," Sanchez recalled about his early days. "It's just the condition that you exist in. In reality, when you look back, there were some pretty tough times. But our mother was very focused on making sure we got our education, and she was a pretty good disciplinarian, too, making sure that we were not messing around and getting into trouble and making sure that we were at school. When we thought otherwise, she had her means of getting us back in line."*

Admiring the Uniform

Sanchez found his way to the military because other members of his family had followed the same path. His father had learned to be a welder while in the service, and his half brothers Ramon and Domingo were in the armed forces as Sanchez grew up. Domingo, who served as an Air Force paratrooper in Vietnam, became an especially big influence in the boy's life. Sanchez began to think seriously about a military career while in junior high school. In high school he joined the Reserve Officer Training Corps (ROTC), in which students train for a future in the armed forces.

Meanwhile, Sanchez didn't ignore his other studies. His good grades made him a member of the National Honor Society, and he graduated eighth in his class at Rio Grande City High School in 1969. His high marks and ROTC studies earned him an Army-Air Force scholarship for college.

——— **"** ———

During the Vietnam War, anti-war protesters directed a lot of anger at Sanchez and other ROTC cadets. "I remember being in altercations with protestors who were trying to take down the flag and burn it," Sanchez said. "We wouldn't allow them to. Sometimes they'd come around during formations and throw tomatoes at us or spit on us."

——— **"** ———

The Vietnam Era

His future looked set except for one thing: the Vietnam War. By 1969, when Sanchez graduated from high school, large numbers of U.S. troops had been fighting in Vietnam for four years, and America had become bitterly divided over the conflict. Following Domingo's example, Sanchez wanted to aid in the fight, but to do so, he would have had to give up his scholarship and enlist immediately as a soldier. In the end, Sanchez opted for college, mostly because of advice he received from Domingo. His older half brother told him to get his education while he had the chance and that "the war would be waiting" for him after he graduated.

Sanchez enrolled at the University of Texas in Austin in the fall of 1969, but his experiences at the state's largest university weren't pleasant. While he was a student there, heated antiwar protests took place on campus. The Vietnam War had a polarizing effect on American society, creating deep divisions between those who supported and those who opposed the war. Sentiment against the war was very intense, especially on college campuses. And some of that anger was directed at Sanchez and other ROTC cadets. "I remember being in altercations with protestors who were trying to take down the flag and burn it," Sanchez said. "We wouldn't allow them to. Sometimes they'd come around during formations and throw tomatoes at us or spit on us."

At the end of his first year, Sanchez transferred to Texas A&M University in Kingsville, which he found much more to his liking. Sanchez described

Sanchez greets soldiers of the 4th Infantry Division, 1-66th Armored Regiment, during an August 2003 visit to their base in Samarra, Iraq.

A&M as "a conservative area, with encouraging, mentoring professors." It was also a smaller school that had fewer antiwar protests. While in Kingsville, Sanchez met Maria Elena Garza (who coincidentally had the same first names as his mother); the two were married shortly after Sanchez received his bachelor's degree in mathematics and history in 1973. Later, after several years of military service, he attended the Naval Postgraduate School in Monterey, California. There, he received a master's degree in operations research and systems analysis engineering. He has also completed courses at the Command and General Staff College and the U.S. Army War College.

CAREER HIGHLIGHTS

As it turned out, Sanchez never got the chance to fight in Vietnam. By the time he graduated from college, U.S. involvement in the conflict was coming to an end. He was still intent on a military career, however. He was commissioned as a second lieutenant in the 82nd Airborne Division of the U.S. Army in 1973 and began his long climb up the ladder of military command.

Between the mid 1970s and the early 1990s, Sanchez was stationed in many different spots in the United States and in foreign countries, includ-

115

ing assignments in Korea, Germany, and Panama. In the course of his career, his family has moved 16 different times. As he advanced through the ranks, Sanchez was one of relatively few Hispanics to become a senior Army officer. He hasn't complained very much about encountering discrimination in the service, but he believes his ethnic background did create some obstacles for him. "You just knew you had to work a little harder if you wanted to succeed," he said of being a Mexican American. "Just performing well wasn't good enough."

> ――― " ―――
>
> *Sanchez was one of relatively few Hispanics to become a senior Army officer. He hasn't complained very much about encountering discrimination in the service, but he believes his ethnic background did create some obstacles for him. "You just knew you had to work a little harder if you wanted to succeed," he said of being a Mexican American. "Just performing well wasn't good enough."*
>
> ――― " ―――

Sanchez specialized in commanding tank battalions, which required him to lead several hundred soldiers at a time. Because the United States wasn't involved in any large wars in the late 1970s and 1980s, most of his assignments didn't involve actual combat missions. Instead, his troops maintained a presence in important areas such as Korea, and they trained hard so that they would be ready to fight when they were called upon. In 1990, they received that call.

The Persian Gulf War

In August 1990, the Iraqi army, commanded by President Saddam Hussein, invaded nearby Kuwait and threatened Saudi Arabia. Hussein was widely considered a brutal, cruel, and ruthless dictator who executed or imprisoned those who challenged his authority. Under his abusive regime, the Iraqi people had few rights and suffered greatly. The Iraqi invasion of Kuwait was considered an act of aggression against a sovereign nation, and the United Nations and the international community were determined to stop it. The UN set a series of deadlines for Iraq to withdraw from Kuwait. At the same time, U.S. President George Bush put together an international coalition to oppose the Iraqi forces, and troops from the U.S. and other countries took up positions in Saudi Arabia. Sanchez and his tank battalion were among them. (For more information on Hussein, see *Biography Today*, July 1992, and Updates in the Annual Cumulations for 1996, 2001, and 2002.)

In January 1991, the U.S. launched Desert Storm, a UN offensive that included more than half a million U.S. troops. The first part of the war was an air offensive that included attacks on Iraqi forces in Kuwait and Iraq, targeting command and control operations. The air offensive lasted five weeks, followed by a ground war. Iraqi troops suffered heavy losses during that part of the war, and in their retreat they set fire to many oil wells, creating massive environmental damage. The Iraqis were forced to surrender after six weeks of war. The war had been swift and devastating, leaving approximately 200,000 dead (mostly Iraqis) and many more displaced from their homes. By the end of the war, UN forces had defeated the Iraqis, but Saddam Hussein was allowed to remain in power. At the time, many questioned whether fighting should have continued until UN forces ousted Hussein from power.

Sanchez and his troops played a part in two important engagements. They came to the aid of an infantry battalion that had run out of fuel in the Iraqi desert, arriving on the scene in the middle of the night to help fight off the enemy. His battalion also attacked Tallil Air Field in southern Iraq. Sanchez's tanks made a daring assault through the main gates of the airfield, braving enemy artillery fire. They captured the airfield and destroyed Iraqi planes and anti-aircraft batteries.

"Your adrenaline is just pumping," Sanchez said of his Gulf War experience. "You don't think about it. You focus on leading your soldiers through the mission and getting them out of there." For his exploits in the war, Sanchez was awarded the Bronze Star with the "V Device" that indicates valor. Following the war, he was promoted to the rank of brigadier general.

Serving in Eastern Europe

Later in the 1990s, Sanchez was involved in another world hotspot—in Kosovo in the Balkan region of Eastern Europe. In the 1990s, the country of Yugoslavia was torn apart by ethnic conflicts among the different peoples living there, including Albanians, Bulgarians, Romanians, Serbs, Croats, Slovenes, Bosnians, Macedonians, Montenegrans, Greeks, and Turks. The wars in the region began in 1991 when the republic of Slovenia declared its independence from Yugoslavia. Other conflicts followed, as other republics within Yugoslavia tried to gain their independence, and Yugoslav forces led by President Slobodan Milosevic fought to stop them. Milosevic and the Serbian troops were widely accused of crimes against humanity, genocide, and ethnic cleansing—the systematic torture and murder to eliminate their enemies, whom they hated solely because of their ethnic group. (For more information on Milosevic, see *Biography*

Sanchez speaks to Albanian soldiers at the Mosul airfield during a visit to the 101st Airborne Division.

Today, Sep. 1999, and Updates in the Annual Cumulations for 2000, 2001, and 2002.)

Fighting in Kosovo, a province of Serbia, started in the summer of 1998, as an armed group of ethnic Albanians fought to win independence from Serbia. The Serbian soldiers attacked civilians, as they had in earlier conflicts in other parts of Yugoslavia. To protect the ethnic Albanians of Kosovo, troops were sent there by the United States and some of its allies from NATO, a military alliance made up of the U.S. and many European countries. Sanchez commanded NATO peacekeeping forces that helped restore order after the Yugoslav army was forced out of Kosovo.

Regardless of where he was stationed, Sanchez earned a reputation for looking out for the soldiers he commanded. One example comes from the Gulf War. In the weeks before the fighting started Sanchez was given the option of making a brief visit home to attend to a family emergency. His commander, Retired General Barry McCaffrey, remembers that he told Sanchez, "we're not going to war in the next 14 days for sure. Go home, get involved in the situation . . . and come back. . . . You're not going to miss the fighting." Sanchez refused to leave. "I'm not going home until I can take my soldiers home," he told McCaffrey. Another of his former commanders, Retired Lieutenant General Randy House, said that "[Sanchez] had a feeling for soldiers that all officers do not have. . . . He could accomplish any mission while always looking out for the benefit of his troops."

In the United States Army, there are several different ranks of generals. When Sanchez first became a general, he was at the lowest rank — a one-star or brigadier general. He later received his second star, becoming a major general. In 2001, while still a two-star general, he was given command of the 1st Armored Division of V Corps, the oldest armored division in the U.S. forces. This put Sanchez in command of more than 10,000 soldiers.

The division soon had to prepare for a new engagement against an old enemy. In 2002 a coalition led by the U.S. and the United Kingdom confronted Iraqi leader Saddam Hussein once again. Alarmed by the possibility that the Iraqi leader was developing nuclear and biological weapons, the coalition demanded that Iraq comply with UN disarmament resolutions. Hussein refused. The U.S. argued that under Hussein, Iraq had developed weapons of mass destruction. Some also questioned whether he had been involved in terrorist activities, including the terrorist attacks of September 11, 2001. Soon, the coalition began massing forces near Iraq. Negotiations and weapons inspections failed to end the standoff, and in March 2003 the Iraq War began. Coalition forces quickly routed the Iraqi Army and took control of the country.

Return to Iraq

In June 2003, just six weeks after major combat operations ended in Iraq, Sanchez received a new promotion. He became a three-star or lieutenant general and was placed in command of the army's V Corps, which included more than 20,000 troops. He was also given a very large responsibility: he was put in charge of all military operations in Iraq.

In some ways, Sanchez's task was just as difficult as that faced by the commanders who had overseen the actual combat operations in Iraq. First of all, the fighting wasn't over. Insurgents opposed to the coalition forces staged attacks on both civilian and military targets. In some cases bombs were planted next to roads, then detonated when military vehicles passed by. The insurgents also used rocket-propelled grenades and car bombs with deadly effect. In August 2003, the number of coalition forces killed by these types of attacks surpassed the number that had been killed in combat operations. The death toll continued to rise in ensuing months.

—————— *"* ——————

Retired Lieutenant General Randy House said that "[Sanchez] had a feeling for soldiers that all officers do not have. . . . He could accomplish any mission while always looking out for the benefit of his troops."

—————— *"* ——————

The situation was made more difficult because Sanchez's troops had to assist in rebuilding the war-torn country. The electrical system had been badly damaged, and the machinery and pipelines used to pump and process oil — Iraq's biggest trade commodity — desperately needed repair. The general also faced a tough political situation. Iraq is made up of several different ethnic groups and religious factions, and there was a danger they

Sanchez walks with Secretary of Defense Donald H. Rumsfeld after his arrival in Baghdad, where he planned to meet with coalition forces.

might begin fighting with one another as they tried to establish their positions in the new nation. Sanchez was honest about the challenges. "We did expect instability before we arrived here," he said, but he also admitted that "we did not expect . . . the political and economic structures to shut down. That was clearly a surprise — at least for me it was." In spite of the difficulties, he remained confident that the coalition forces could not be beaten in battle by the insurgents. "The stark reality is that they cannot defeat us, and they know it. I am supremely confident of this reality."

The Search for Weapons

In addition to their other duties, the coalition forces searched the country for the weapons of mass destruction that the Iraqis were believed to possess. After months of hunting for evidence of chemical and nuclear weapons, the coalition forces found no weapons of mass destruction. This led some people in the U.S. and other countries to criticize the invasion of Iraq: the weapons of mass destruction had been the main reason for going to war, and now they couldn't be found. In fact, it wasn't clear that Iraq had possessed any such weapons. When Sanchez was asked whether he believed that Saddam had such weapons, he replied "That's a question I can't answer."

Even after the war ended, fighting continued in Iraq and U.S. troops continued to die. Some people began to compare the engagement to the Vietnam War, where U.S. forces had become involved in a prolonged conflict that they had difficulty winning or ending. Sanchez felt such comparisons were totally wrong. "It's not Vietnam," he said, "and there's no way you can make the comparison to the quagmire of Vietnam, when you look at the progress that's being made." The general went out of his way to point out the positive things that were happening in Iraq. "The progress is unbelievable. We just have to make sure that the American public realizes that and understands that their sons and daughters are making a tremendous contribution to the peace and stability and the democratic future of Iraq."

Where's Hussein?

When coalition forces took over Iraq in April 2003, they toppled Saddam Hussein's government, but Hussein himself had escaped capture. So had his sons and some other key figures in the government. In the months that followed, Sanchez directed his troops to hunt these people down. In July 2003, U.S. troops killed Saddam's two sons, Uday and Qusay Hussein, in the town of Mosul. Still, Saddam Hussein remained on the loose.

Sanchez believed that finding the former dictator was crucial because it would show Iraqis that Hussein could never return to power. Also, it might discourage the insurgents who were attacking coalition forces. In the fall of 2003, the hunt was still on. When Sanchez was asked how close he had come to capturing Saddam, he replied "not close enough. I don't know how close I've got to him, but by God I've got to get closer."

Soon he did. On December 13, U.S. forces searched an area around a mud hut near the town of Tikrit. In a hidden underground room that the soldiers called a "spider hole" they found Hussein. He was captured without a fight and transferred to a detention facility. There, Sanchez had his first

> "
>
> *Sanchez was honest about the challenges in Iraq. "We did expect instability before we arrived here, . . . [but we did not expect] the political and economic structures to shut down. That was clearly a surprise — at least for me it was." Yet he remained confident that the coalition forces could not be beaten in battle by the insurgents. "The stark reality is that they cannot defeat us, and they know it. I am supremely confident of this reality."*
>
> "

face-to-face meeting with the former dictator. Hussein was now a bearded and bedraggled figure who looked as if he had suffered during his months on the run. "It was sobering to be able to stand in the presence of a man that was such a brutal dictator," Sanchez said of the meeting, "and to ensure that he's no longer going to abuse his people." Sanchez didn't feel that Hussein's capture was going to end the armed opposition in Iraq, but he did see it as a step in the right direction. "I think what we've accomplished clearly by arresting Saddam is that we've eliminated the source of fear that has pervaded across Iraq for at least 35 years, and that still continued to hinder our progress toward safety and stability."

> ── " ──
>
> "I think what we've accomplished clearly by arresting Saddam is that we've eliminated the source of fear that has pervaded across Iraq for at least 35 years, and that still continued to hinder our progress toward safety and stability."
>
> ── " ──

New Challenges

As Sanchez predicted, the dangers faced by coalition forces continued. Insurgent attacks continued through the early months of 2004, and the situation got worse in April. That month, 139 soldiers from the U.S. and its allies were killed. Many of them died in terrorist-style attacks, but there was also a pitched battle in the town of Fallujah. After laying siege to the town, coalition troops withdrew without ousting the insurgents based there. Sanchez had his hands full with the ongoing attacks and the many problems involved in managing affairs in Iraq. But then in May 2004, he faced a challenge of a different kind. It proved to be the most serious of his command.

A series of news stories revealed that U.S. troops had been involved in the mistreatment of Iraqi prisoners. The news stories were accompanied by very disturbing photos of U.S. troops abusing the prisoners. The incidents had taken place at Abu Ghraib (*a-boo GRAAYB*) prison near Baghdad between October and December of 2003. Prisoners had been beaten, deprived of clothing, forced to pose in humiliating positions, and threatened and attacked by guard dogs. One prisoner was killed while in custody. These actions were violations of the Geneva Conventions, a series of specific guidelines created by the international community that govern the way prisoners of war should be treated. Some of the U.S. soldiers involved said they had treated the prisoners badly so the Iraqis would give information to military intelligence interrogators.

Sanchez reviewing Iraqi troops on parade.

The photos created an uproar in the United States and all around the world. President Bush and many other U.S. officials had repeatedly said that the war in Iraq would help the Iraqi people. The stories of abuse cast doubt on those claims and made the U.S. presence in Iraq less popular among Americans. Seven soldiers faced criminal charges for their role in the mistreatment, but the story didn't end with them. There were suspicions that those charged were following orders from superior officers.

Facing Questions

Because he was the senior commander in Iraq, Sanchez faced tough questions about what had happened at Abu Ghraib. He was called to Washington, D.C., to testify before the Senate Armed Services Committee. He reported that he had first learned of the abuse in January 2004 and had launched an investigation soon afterward. (That investigation became the basis of the news stories that appeared several months later.) While few people believed that Sanchez had a direct role in the prisoner mistreatment, he had issued an order in mid November 2003 that placed Abu Ghraib under the command of military intelligence personnel. Some people believed that this change had set the stage for the abuse.

In July 2004, Sanchez stepped down as the senior commander in Iraq and was replaced by General George Casey Jr. When the change was announced in late May, senior U.S. officials claimed that the change had nothing to do with the Abu Ghraib incident. Secretary of State Colin Powell said that replacing Sanchez was part of "the normal scheme of things," and President Bush stated that Sanchez had "done a fabulous job" in Iraq. Other observers, however, felt that the reassignment had been partly caused by the prison controversy. After turning over command to Casey, Sanchez admitted that "Abu Ghraib was a great defeat for the coalition here in this country." Sanchez has made few other comments to the press, but his wife, Maria Elena, said that the general isn't shaken by the controversy. "He's not worried, " she said, "because he has nothing to be ashamed of and nothing to regret." She also reported that Sanchez had told her, "don't worry, they will find out. The truth will come out." The general's next assignment has yet to be decided.

> ———— **"** ————
>
> *Sanchez feels that U.S. forces have a very good chance of succeeding, as long as people in the United States remain committed to the mission. "I really believe that the only way we are going to lose here is if we walk away from it like we did in Vietnam. . . . If the political will fails and the support of the American public fails, that's the only way we can lose."*
>
> ———— **"** ————

Whatever the ultimate outcome of events, Sanchez has expressed a strong commitment to the U.S. mission in Iraq. This is partly due to similarities he noticed between the tough conditions in Iraq and those he experienced as a boy. "At times I fly around and see situations that remind me of the tough times that I went through, some of the poverty. . . . I sometimes see myself in the kids that are out there." He believes that the intervention of the coalition forces will do a lot to help those young people and that the U.S. has done "absolutely the right thing for this country by having gotten rid of Saddam." He also feels that U.S. forces have a very good chance of succeeding, as long as people in the United States remain committed to the mission. "I really believe that the only way we are going to lose here is if we walk away from it like we did in Vietnam. . . . If the political will fails and the support of the American public fails, that's the only way we can lose."

*A change of command ceremony at Al-Faw Palace in Baghdad, July 1, 2004:
Lt. General Ricardo Sanchez (left), outgoing Commanding General of Coalition
Forces in Iraq; General John P. Abizaid (center), Commanding General of U.S.
Central Command; and General George W. Casey (right), incoming
Commanding General of Coalition Forces in Iraq.*

Being a Role Model

As the highest-ranking Hispanic in the U.S. Army and only the ninth
Hispanic general in the army's history, Sanchez has become an important
role model for many young Hispanic soldiers. When asked about his will-
ingness to be a role model, Sanchez answered without hesitation:
"Absolutely. Whether you like it or not, once you are honored with these
kinds of responsibilities, and more importantly blessed by all those great
people over the years who allowed you to succeed, it's inevitable that you
will be looked at as a role model. There's a tremendous responsibility that
goes along with it. Primarily, it's making sure that at every opportunity you
can engage with young people and share with them some of the difficulties
and successes and maybe even some of the breaks that allowed you to succeed." The accusations about the scandal at Abu Ghraib prison have made
his status as a role model more problematic. Still, many are glad to see a
Hispanic leader attain a position of such authority.

MAJOR INFLUENCES

Sanchez has made it clear that his mother was the greatest influence on
his life and his values. "She was very disciplined and focused and taught

125

"She was very disciplined and focused and taught us about perseverance and dedication and definitely about family,"Sanchez said about his mother. "Those are the values the Hispanic community embraces. It's patriotism, service to country, and being very loyal to your family. When I became a soldier, the ethics and the value system of the military profession fit almost perfectly with that ethic. It made it very easy for me to adapt to the military value system."

————— " —————

us about perseverance and dedication and definitely about family," he recalls of her firm approach. "Those are the values the Hispanic community embraces. It's patriotism, service to country, and being very loyal to your family. When I became a soldier, the ethics and the value system of the military profession fit almost perfectly with that ethic. It made it very easy for me to adapt to the military value system."

MARRIAGE AND FAMILY

Sanchez met his wife, Maria Elena Garza (she has the same first name as Sanchez's mother), while attending college in Kingsville, Texas, and they were married in December 1973. Sanchez has said that his wife is "my best friend and my greatest supporter. . . . She's just made so many sacrifices for me and my family. She's the reason I am a general today." The Sanchezes have four children, two boys and two girls; a fifth child died in a car accident.

HOBBIES AND OTHER INTERESTS

In his spare time, Sanchez likes to jog and play racquetball and tennis. He also enjoys studying military history.

HONORS AND AWARDS

Distinguished Alumni Award (Texas A&M University): 2003
Hispanic of the Year (*Hispanic* magazine): 2003
Army Commendation Medal
Army Achievement Medal with Oak Leaf Cluster
Bronze Star with "V" Device and Oak Leaf Cluster
Defense Superior Service Medal
Joint Service Commendation Medal

Legion of Merit
Liberation of Kuwait Medals (Saudi Arabia and Kuwait)
Master Parachutist Badge
Meritorious Service Medal with Four Oak Leaf Clusters
Southwest Asia Campaign Medal

FURTHER READING

Periodicals

Chicago Tribune, Oct. 20, 2003, p.CN1
Corpus Christi (Tex.) Caller-Times, Dec. 21, 2003, p.A1; May 26, 2004, p.A1
Hispanic, Dec. 2003, pp.8 and 44
International Herald Tribune (Paris), Jan. 12, 2004, p.2
Los Angeles Times, Sept. 14, 2003, p.A10
New York Times, Nov. 12, 2003, p.A8; Dec. 15, 2003, p.A18; May 9, 2004, section 1, p.1
San Antonio Express-News, June 23, 2003, p.A1; Dec. 28, 2003, p.A1
USA Today, May 26, 2004, p.A5

Online Articles

http://www.cnn.com/SPECIALS/2003/iraq
  (CNN.com "War in Iraq," undated)

ADDRESS

Lt. General Ricardo Sanchez
V Corps, U.S. Army
Römerstrasse 168
Geb. # D-69126
Heidelberg, Germany

WORLD WIDE WEB SITE

http://www.vcorps.army.mil/Leaders/LTGS.htm

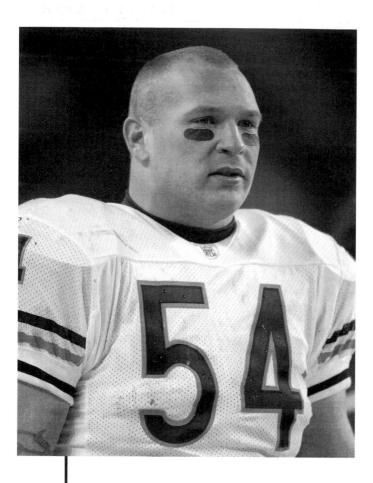

Brian Urlacher 1978-

American Professional Football Player with the
Chicago Bears
NFL Defensive Player of the Year for 2001

BIRTH

Brian Keith Urlacher (pronounced *UR-LACK-ER*) was born on
May 25, 1978, in Pasco, Washington. He weighed a whopping
11 pounds, 8 ounces at birth — an early clue that he was going
to be big. Brian is the son of Brad Urlacher and Lavoyda (Bee-
man) Urlacher. His parents divorced when he was in elementary school, and Brian saw little of his biological father after

that. He was raised by his mother and his stepfather, Troy Lenard. Brian has an older sister, Sheri, and a younger brother, Casey.

YOUTH

Brian spent his early years in Washington State. When his parents divorced in the mid-1980s, the children remained with their mother. In 1986 Lavoyda Urlacher decided to move the family to Lovington, New Mexico, where her parents lived. Brian spent the rest of his youth in Lovington, a small town of about 9,000 people in the southeastern part of the state, near the Texas-New Mexico border. His father remained in Washington and had little contact with his children after they moved to New Mexico.

The family did not have much money. Lavoyda was sometimes forced to work several jobs in order to make ends meet. In fact, she once held three different jobs at the same time — at a grocery store, a convenience store, and a laundry. "We ate a lot of macaroni and cheese during that time," Lavoyda recalled, "but the kids never went without. I had energy and desire, and I swore we were going to make it one way or another." Busy as she was, Lavoyda still found time to enroll her children in sporting activities and attended as many of their games as she could. Brian and Casey, who are just a year apart in age, became obsessed with sports, competing in everything from basketball to baseball to football to swimming.

——— " ———

Urlacher's family did not have much money, and his mother worked several jobs in order to make ends meet. "We ate a lot of macaroni and cheese during that time," she recalled, "but the kids never went without. I had energy and desire, and I swore we were going to make it one way or another."

——— " ———

A New Dad

For several years the Urlacher children missed having a father in their lives. Then, in 1992, Lavoyda married a man named Troy Lenard. Lenard had a son of his own and worked in the oilfields that surround Lovington. The Urlacher children had no trouble accepting their new stepfather's presence in their lives. "Troy stood right in for our biological father," Brian recalled. "To this day we consider him our real dad. . . . Just like my mom, he took care of us."

129

Though Troy and Lavoyda later divorced, Lenard was there at a key time for Brian. He provided a sense of discipline for a boy who was just entering his teenage years. Though he was not overly strict, Troy let the children know that if they got out of line, they risked a meeting with "Uncle Henry" — a board that Troy threatened to use as a paddle. The mere threat was usually enough to make the boys behave. In fact, Troy recalled that he only paddled the boys once: "I made them grab their ankles, they got one swat, and that was it."

In most cases, though, Brian did not require any kind of punishment. His mother had laid down the law very clearly even before Troy was around. If Brian seriously misbehaved — by cutting classes or drinking alcohol, for instance — he would not be allowed to play sports. This was a threat far more terrifying than Uncle Henry, so Brian followed the rules. In fact, the only heavy drinking that Brian did in high school was downing lots and lots of chocolate milk.

—————— " ——————

"Casey could always stay right with me in everything," Urlacher remembered. *"It felt more like we were competitors sharing the same house than like we were brothers."*

—————— " ——————

Like many brothers, Brian and Casey became strong rivals, always trying to outdo one another. This was true when they were competing on the field, and even when they went fishing or lifted weights. Their competition became so intense that it sometimes seemed as if the boys really disliked one another. Their mother started signing Brian and Casey up for separate teams to help create a little breathing room between them. "Casey could always stay right with me in everything," Brian remembered. "It felt more like we were competitors sharing the same house than like we were brothers."

EDUCATION

Urlacher attended public schools in Lovington, where he earned mostly As and Bs. Not surprisingly, playing on the school athletic teams was very important to him. By the time he got to high school, his favorite sports were football and basketball. He played both of these sports for the Lovington Wildcats, as well as being a member of the track team.

Though he was very large as a baby and eventually became a big, imposing football player, Urlacher was a rather normal-sized teenager during his first years in high school. As a freshman, he stood about 5 feet, 10 inches tall and weighed around 160 pounds. Fortunately, he was not done growing. In his final two years he shot up to 6 feet, 3 inches and packed on an additional 50 pounds. Most of the new weight was muscle, as Urlacher launched an intensive weight-training program at the suggestion of one of the Wildcat football coaches. He had always been a fast runner, and he lost none of his quickness as he got larger, posting an impressive time of 4.57 seconds in the 40-yard dash. This combination of strength and speed has been the key to Urlacher's success.

Hometown Star

Urlacher started his high school football career as a wide receiver. But as his size and skills increased, he played a lot of different roles for the Wildcats, including safety on defense, receiver and running back on offense, and kick returner on special teams. With his help, Lovington became one of the best teams in the state of New Mexico. The Wildcats made it to the division AAA state championship in his junior year, but lost.

In Urlacher's senior year, the team went undefeated in the regular season and once again reached the championship game. The Wildcats took a 14-7 lead late in the game. Then, in a moment that became legendary in Lovington, Urlacher made a leaping interception to seal the game and claim the state title for the Wildcats. He finished his senior year with 61 catches for 15 touchdowns, and he added a total of eight more touchdowns through rushing, punt returns, and kickoff returns. Urlacher received all-state honors as both a wide receiver and a safety.

Even though he was the star of his high school football team, Urlacher did not receive much attention from college recruiters—partly because Lovington High was a small school. He dreamed of attending Texas Tech, which was located just 100 miles from Lovington, but the university did not offer him a scholarship. As it turned out, the University of New Mexico (UNM) in Albuquerque was the only major college to offer him an athletic scholarship, and he was not even considered one of their hottest prospects. In fact, the university sent an assistant coach to meet with Urlacher because, as he recalled, "I wasn't a big enough recruit for the head coach to visit."

Still, Urlacher was grateful for the opportunity to attend college and continue to play football. "I'm just glad someone found me," he said. "The chance I got from New Mexico was a blessing." After graduating from high school in 1996, Urlacher packed his bags and moved to Albuquerque. He majored in criminology at UNM, but he did not complete his degree. He

Urlacher was a star defensive back during his colllege days playing for the University of New Mexico Lobos.

stopped attending classes following his final season of college football, as he was preparing to begin his NFL career.

CAREER HIGHLIGHTS

College — The University of New Mexico Lobos

Urlacher's college football career with the UNM Lobos got off to a rather slow start. During his freshman season in 1996, he failed to make the starting defensive squad and played mostly on the kicking teams. Although he was not yet making a big splash on the field, Urlacher continued to work hard. "I just feel like I always have something to prove," he explained. "If you have that attitude throughout your career, I think you're always going to do well because you're going to work harder than everybody else." Urlacher spent many hours in the weight room, bulking up to 235 pounds. He also grew another inch to reach his current height of 6 feet, 4 inches. His growth caused a sensation when he returned to Lovington following his first year of college. "I didn't recognize him," recalled a friend of the Urlacher family. "I couldn't find his neck."

Like most new college students, Urlacher had to adjust to being away from his home and family. He found it most difficult to be separated from his brother Casey, even though their sibling rivalry had led to numerous fights over the years. "Until Casey wasn't around anymore, I didn't realize how much I could miss someone and how much they could mean to me," Urlacher said.

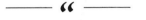

"I just feel like I always have something to prove," Urlacher explained. "If you have that attitude throughout your career, I think you're always going to do well because you're going to work harder than everybody else."

During his sophomore season in 1997, Urlacher still did not make the starting lineup. But he did see a lot of action at linebacker (a defensive position in which the player lines up behind the line of scrimmage and is responsible for both pass and run defense). Ranking second on the team in tackles by season's end, he was beginning to show his skills. The Lobos had a good season that year, winning nine games and going to the Insight.com Bowl, where they lost to Arizona.

Prior to Urlacher's junior year UNM got a new head coach, Rocky Long, who decided to reorganize the team's defense. In fact, Long decided to

133

make Urlacher the centerpiece of the new design. Instead of playing as a standard linebacker, Urlacher was moved to the "Lobo back" position — a combination of free safety and linebacker. From his position about ten yards behind the line of scrimmage, he could defend against passes and also pursue rushers carrying the ball. As Coach Long explained it, the new defense "allowed Brian a chance to be in on every play."

The new position was perfectly matched to Urlacher's skills, and he wasted no time in making his mark. He racked up 178 tackles for the 1998 season, the highest total in the nation. His outstanding defensive production continued in his senior season, when he tallied 154 tackles to rank fourth in the nation. Over the course of these two seasons, Urlacher went from a mostly unknown second stringer to one of the best defensive players in the country. He also continued to demonstrate his versatility on the field. He returned punts and kickoffs for the Lobos and, in his senior year, occasionally played as an offensive receiver, scoring six touchdowns. Unfortunately, UNM posted losing seasons in both Urlacher's junior and senior years.

> "This kind of thing had never happened to me before," Urlacher said of his early struggles as an NFL rookie. "I was so disappointed. I was down on myself, and I wasn't sure what I could do to get myself playing again."

At the close of his last college season, Urlacher was named to several All-America teams and was one of three finalists for the Jim Thorpe Award, which is presented each year to the best defensive back in the country. He even finished 12th in the voting for the prestigious Heisman Trophy, which honors the best college football player of the year.

NFL — The Chicago Bears

Urlacher's performance impressed many professional football scouts. When the 2000 NFL draft took place in April, he was selected ninth overall by the Chicago Bears. He soon signed a five-year contract that paid him $13 million. Urlacher knew that he might have received a larger contract if he would have extended the negotiations, but he was eager to start playing football. "I want to be with my teammates from the beginning," he said, meaning that he did not want to miss training camp by holding off on signing his contract. "And I don't want to disappoint the fans."

Urlacher tackles New York Giants wide receiver Ike Hilliard in action from his rookie season.

At first Urlacher had trouble adjusting to the fact that he was suddenly a millionaire. Shortly before the draft he had admitted, "I think a hundred dollars is a lot of money." That attitude did not change quickly after his big payday. In fact, the first meal he ate after signing his contract was not at a fancy restaurant, but at McDonald's.

Unfortunately, the transition to the NFL did not go smoothly for Urlacher. Unlike UNM, the Bears did not design a special defense around him. Instead, Urlacher had to play as a true linebacker—up close to the line of scrimmage. He started out as the team's strong-side linebacker, meaning that it was usually his responsibility to match up against the offensive tight end. It was a position he had no experience with, and he had difficulty adjusting. "Most of what I'm learning now, it's all new," he admitted in an early training camp. "I screw up every play just about."

Urlacher also found that the speed of the professional game was much different from what he had experienced in college. "Here everything is much faster, especially being close to the line of scrimmage," he explained. "You don't have as much time to react because the linemen are on you so quick." On top of everything else, Urlacher faced the pressure of trying to fill the shoes of some of the great linebackers who had played for the Chicago Bears in the past, including Dick Butkus and Mike Singletary.

Even before preseason, the Bears had announced that Urlacher would start on defense. But the coaches grew discouraged by the troubles he was having. Just before the regular season got underway, Urlacher was demoted and another player took over his starting spot. "This kind of thing had never happened to me before," he said. "I was so disappointed. I was down on myself, and I wasn't sure what I could do to get myself playing again." As it turned out, all he could do was wait for another chance. Fortunately, the wait was short.

Before the third game of the season, the Bears' starting middle linebacker, Barry Minter, was injured. Urlacher took over the position, and suddenly everything clicked. In his first game in this new position, he racked up 13 tackles and one quarterback sack. He had found his place, and he was not about to give it up. Minter never got his starting job back. "I needed more space to roam," Urlacher said of playing in the middle. "I was too confined at outside linebacker." By the close of the 2000 season he had notched 165 tackles, eight sacks, and two interceptions. He was voted the NFL Defensive Rookie of the Year and played in the Pro Bowl. In just 14 games, Urlacher had proven himself one of the best linebackers in the business.

In the Spotlight

During the off-season following his stellar rookie year, Urlacher made a brief visit to Lovington for a special occasion: his high school football and basketball jerseys were retired in a half-time ceremony at a Wildcats basketball game. He also became the first inductee into the Lovington Hall of Fame. To his hometown, Urlacher had already become a legend. Josh Faith, the son of the high school football coach, said that Urlacher's success "lifts the whole town up because he's a Lovington product. It makes us all feel good. It shows us that dreams really do come true, and if you set your mind to it, you can do anything." The visit brought back fond memories for Urlacher. "It's the same way as when I left it," he said of Lovington. "That's why I like it. It will always be the way I left it." In appreciation of the help he got from his high school, Urlacher donated warm-up suits and other equipment for the sports teams.

The honors he received in Lovington were an early sign that Urlacher was becoming famous — and not just in his hometown. The city of Chicago needed just one season to go crazy over Urlacher, and the attention he received there and all around the country grew more intense over the next few years. At one point in 2002, replicas of his jersey outsold those of all other players in the NFL. Urlacher has never been the type to bask in the spotlight, and he sometimes had difficulty dealing with his fame. "Man, I'll

Urlacher scored the winning touchdown on a fake field goal in this 2001 game against the Washington Redskins.

never get used to it," he said of the endless interviews with reporters. "They always ask the same questions over and over again."

Fame also made it more difficult for him to do simple things like go out to a restaurant for dinner. He found that he had to choose the places he appeared in public carefully, and he often wore a hat to avoid being recognized. On the other hand, Urlacher willingly devoted a lot of time to sign-

In 2001 Urlacher earned NFL Defensive Player of the Year honors.

ing autographs. He realized that without sports fans, he would not get paid to play football. "The people are coming out here . . . to see you," he said. "They expect you to give something back to them, which I don't mind doing." He was especially happy to give his autograph to young fans. "I'll sign for kids all day long," he stated. But he found some grown-up autograph hounds less to his liking. "When you see the adults pushing the kids out of the way, it kind of makes you mad," he acknowledged.

Winning and Losing with the Bears

Urlacher's emergence as one of the league's best linebackers was one of the few bright spots for the Bears in 2000. The team finished with just five wins that year, and they were not expected to fare much better the following season. But the 2001 season turned out to be a pleasant surprise for Chicago. With an explosive offense and a tough defense anchored by Urlacher, the team posted a 13-3 record and won the NFC Central Division. They faced the Philadelphia Eagles in the playoffs, but were beaten 33-13. Urlacher posted 148 tackles, 6 sacks, and 3 interceptions for the year. He even scored two touchdowns: one by running back a fumble he recovered, and the other by catching a pass on a fake field-goal play. Urlacher led all defensive players in fan voting for the Pro Bowl, and he was named the NFL Defensive Player of the Year by *Football Digest*.

> **"**
>
> *"It makes things easier for me and my family, I know that much," Urlacher said about his many endorsement deals. "And that's really what it comes down to in life, I think, is how well you take care of yourself and your family. But we don't flaunt it or anything like that."*
>
> **"**

The Bears entered the 2002 season with high hopes. But many key players went down with injuries, and Chicago finished with just four wins for the year. Though he was disappointed with his team's record, Urlacher posted the best numbers of his career. He tallied 17 tackles in the opening game against the Minnesota Vikings, and his season total of 214 set a new record for the Bears, breaking the mark held by Dick Butkus for 30 years.

Given Urlacher's performance and popularity, it was clear that his next contract was going to make him very wealthy. Many wondered if he would become a free agent when his contract expired, so he would be able to field offers from other NFL teams. But Urlacher claimed that he wanted to stay in Chicago. "I can't imagine playing anywhere else," he said. "Never." Although his initial contract extended through the 2005 season, the Bears were so eager to hang onto their star that they began negotiating with Urlacher early. Before the 2003 season began, he signed a new deal worth $56 million over nine years.

Thanks to his popularity, Urlacher was able to supplement his income by signing endorsement deals with a number of companies, including Nike, Sega, Campbell's Soup, and Cadillac. "It makes things easier for me and my family, I know that much," he admitted. "And that's really what it comes down to in life, I think, is how well you take care of yourself and your family. But we don't flaunt it or anything like that." Urlacher had long been known as a humble and down-to-earth person, and he was determined to stay that way. "I like to think of myself as a regular guy, except I play football for a living," he explained. "I try not to be an arrogant turd out there."

> "I've seen [Urlacher] take on linemen and drive them into the backfield," declared teammate Mike Brown. "I've seen him hit fullbacks and stop them cold. I've seen him run down running backs from behind. I've seen him cover wide receivers. Who else can do all those things?"

Unfortunately, the Bears had another disappointing season in 2003, finishing 7-9. Head coach Dick Jauron—the only NFL coach Urlacher had known—was fired at the end of the season and replaced by Lovie Smith. Although Urlacher had a good year by most linebackers' standards, racking up 153 tackles, his production declined from the previous year. He also failed to cause a fumble or make an interception all season long.

If his past accomplishments are any indication, Urlacher will certainly be working as hard as he can to put Chicago back on the winning track. "The reason I'm here is because of my work ethic," he stated. "I've always had it instilled in me that you have to work hard if you want something." This attitude has contributed to his reputation as one of the top linebackers in the league. Mike Brown, who has played beside Urlacher in the Bears defense, has witnessed the linebacker's talents at close range: "I've seen him take on linemen and drive them into the backfield," Brown noted. "I've seen him hit fullbacks and stop them cold. I've seen him run down running backs from behind. I've seen him cover wide receivers. Who else can do all those things?"

MARRIAGE AND FAMILY

Urlacher married Laurie Faulhaber in 2000. They have a daughter named Pamela, who was born in December of that year. The family lives in Lake

Urlacher pressures Green Bay quarterback Brett Favre in 2003 action.

Bluff, Illinois, a suburb north of Chicago. Their home features a first-class game room and big-screen television in the basement.

Laurie has described Urlacher as "an amazing father," and there are many accounts of his devotion to his family. As a result, many fans were shocked when he filed for divorce in the spring of 2003. That September, he was spotted at a Las Vegas nightclub with model and celebrity Paris Hilton. A short time later, Hilton sat in Urlacher's skybox during a Bears home game. But Urlacher insisted that reports of a romance between them were exaggerated. "You're seen with someone and all of a sudden you're getting married to them," he said. "It's unbelievable. Things get blown out of proportion so bad." While Urlacher and his wife subsequently tried to reconcile, they ultimately decided to divorce.

Urlacher remains close to his parents and his brother and sister. Once he signed his first NFL contract, he used some of the money to show them his appreciation. He bought every member of his family a new car, for example, and purchased a ranch in Texas for Troy Lenard. He also brought his brother Casey to Illinois and helped him enroll at Lake Forest College. Casey lived with his older brother and played football for Lake Forest until his graduation in 2002.

HOBBIES AND OTHER INTERESTS

Urlacher had been an enthusiastic ping-pong player since he was young, and also enjoys playing air hockey. He likes to relax while listening to music, especially by pop groups like N'Sync and the Backstreet Boys.

HONORS AND AWARDS

First Team Collegiate Football All-American (Football Writers Association of America): 1999
First Team Collegiate Football All-American (Associated Press): 1999
Brian Piccolo Award (Chicago Bears): 2000
NFL Defensive Rookie of the Year (Associated Press): 2000
NFL Rookie of the Year (*Sporting News*): 2000
NFL Pro Bowl: 2000-2003
Unsung Hero Award (NFL Players Association): 2000
All-Pro Team (Associated Press): 2001-2002
NFL Defensive Player of the Year (*Football Digest*): 2001

FURTHER READING

Books

Urlacher: Windy City Warrior, 2002

Periodicals

Albuquerque Journal, Jan. 13, 2002, p.D1
Chicago, Aug. 2002, p.78
Chicago Tribune, Apr. 24, 2000; Feb. 12, 2001, p.N1; Aug. 1, 2001, p.N1; Dec. 9, 2001; Aug. 8, 2002, p.N10
Dallas Morning News, Apr. 13, 2000, p.B13
Denver Post, Aug. 9, 2002, p.D1
New York Times, Jan. 15, 2002, p.D5
Sporting News, Mar. 27, 2000, p.18; Aug. 6, 2001, p.10; Nov. 5, 2001, p.42
Sports Illustrated, May 8, 2000; Oct. 29, 2001, p.50; Sep. 23, 2002, p.52

ADDRESS

Brian Urlacher
The Chicago Bears
Halas Hall
1000 Football Drive
Lake Forest, IL 60045

WORLD WIDE WEB SITES

http://www.brianurlacher.com
http://www.nfl.com/players
http://www.nflplayers.com
http://www.chicagobears.com/team

Michelle Wie 1989-
American Golf Prodigy

BIRTH

Michelle Sung Wie (pronounced *wee*) was born on October 11, 1989, in Honolulu, Hawaii. Her parents, Hyun Kyong (Bo) Wie and Byung-Wook (B.J.) Wie, immigrated to the United States from Korea in the 1980s. Her mother, Bo Wie, is a real estate agent in Honolulu and a Korean amateur golf champion. Her father, B.J. Wie, is a professor at the University of Honolulu and also an accomplished golfer, a skill he learned from his wife. They also help manage their daughter's career. Michelle is their only child.

YOUTH

Wie began hitting a golf ball at age four with a set of junior clubs, smacking her first shot more than 100 yards. She fell in love with the game, playing for hours on end. She played her first round of golf—the complete 18 holes—at age seven, finishing 14 strokes over par. Soon Wie could beat her parents. "I think I started beating them when I was seven or eight," she once said. "Well, they say I . . . started beating them when I was nine, but I refuse to believe that."

In golf scoring, "par" refers to the standard number of strokes it should take a player to complete each hole. For example, most golf courses include short holes, which are usually designated as "par 3," as well as longer holes, which are designated "par 5." On a regulation, 18-hole golf course, par for all holes will add up to 72. In golf terminology, a player makes a "birdie" by completing a hole in one shot under par, or a "bogey" by completing a hole in one shot over par.

By age nine, Wie played her first sub-par round, meaning she was able to complete the 18 holes with fewer shots than expected—in fact, fewer shots than most adults would require for that course. Since then, she has never shot more than 100 for 18 holes of golf. At the same time, Wie began competing in tournaments, winning five out of the seven Oahu Junior Golf Association tournaments at age nine. Through all this time, Wie combined her childhood activities with her dedication to golf.

EARLY CAREER

By this point, Wie was already on the way to become a professional golfer. Professional golfers typically compete in a series of events over the course of the year. The winners of the events can earn big monetary prizes. These events, or tournaments, are offered by golf associations. There are several associations around the world, but in the U.S. the most prestigious for professional golfers are the LPGA (Ladies Professional Golf Association) for women and the PGA (Professional Golf Association) for men.

Most golf tournaments take place over a series of days. Each day, the players shoot one "round" of 18 holes. Players have to make the cut in order to continue in a tournament, or else they are eliminated. The "cut" is the score, set by tournament officials, that players must beat after two rounds to continue. After several rounds, the scores are totaled and the player with the lowest score wins the tournament. There are many individual tournaments on the women's professional golf tour, but the most prestigious are the four major or "Grand Slam" events: the Kraft Nabisco Championship, the U.S. Women's Open, the McDonald's LPGA Championship, and the Weetabix Women's British Open.

In addition to the events for professional golfers, there are tournaments offered for amateur golfers, who do not earn prize money. There are also junior golfer programs, designed to introduce kids to golf. At all these levels, players can qualify for golf events based on their scores and their performance in other tournaments.

Most golfers spend years developing their skills in the amateur ranks, and very few ever learn to play at such advanced levels. What's amazing about Wie is that she has become so accomplished at such a young age.

―――― " ――――

"I think I started beating [my parents] when I was seven or eight," Wie once said. "Well, they say I . . . started beating them when I was nine, but I refuse to believe that."

―――― " ――――

Getting Started

In 2000, at age 10, Wie became the youngest girl to qualify for a USGA amateur championship event. (The United States Golf Association, or USGA, is the national governing body of golf.) At the USGA Women's Amateur Public Links Championship, Wie attained the impressive score of 64. At age 10, she had already developed her game enough to compete in this championship against some of the best women amateurs. Her game so impressed Bev Kim and Lily Yao, two of the top women's amateurs, that they began mentoring her. In 2002, at age 12, Wie became the youngest player ever to qualify for an LPGA event, shooting an 83 to qualify for the LPGA Takefuji Classic. That same year, she became the youngest semi-finalist at the U.S. Women's Amateur Public Links Championship.

The year 2003 brought continued success, as she played in both women's and men's events. She started the year by trying to qualify for the PGA Sony Open, a men's event that was being held in Hawaii. In this and several other events she was granted an exemption—a tournament sponsor's invitation to try to make the cut into the tournament without completing all of the qualifying rounds. She shot a 73 and finished 47 out of 97 in the event—at the age of 13. It was considered a remarkable achievement, and people in the golf world started to take notice. She next played in the Hawaii Pearl Open, a professional men's tournament with players from the Japan Tour. The only female in the tournament, she placed 43rd. She

Despite her youth, Wie's golf game is incredibly well-rounded and complete.

followed that event with an appearance in her first LPGA major tournament, the Kraft Nabisco Championship. Playing against such accomplished golfers as Patricia Meunier-Lebouc and Annika Sorenstam, Wie ended up in ninth place. Her play included a round of 66, which tied the lowest score by an amateur in an LPGA major. In addition, she was the youngest player ever to make the cut at an LPGA event.

Her next event in 2003 was another appearance at the U.S. Women's Amateur Public Links Championship. At just 13 years old, Wie won the tournament, taking her first national title. In the process, she also became the youngest champion of the event and the youngest player ever to win an adult national event.

Wie next appeared at the Canadian Tour's Bay Mills Open Players' Championships, held in Michigan. In her first professional men's event in the mainland United States, she shot 74-79, missing the cut by five strokes. Another men's event followed: the Albertsons Boise Open on the Nationwide Tour, a development tour (like the minor leagues) for the PGA. She shot 78-76 in that event and missed the cut. Her final major event for 2003 was the LPGA Safeway Classic. She shot 69-72-73, or two under par, tying for 28th place. Overall for 2003, she qualified for five out of the six LPGA

Wie follows the flight of her ball after a towering tee shot.

events she entered. And while she had not made the cut in the professional men's tournaments she entered, she had gained experience and exposure.

Playing in the 2004 Sony Open

In early 2004, Wie got an opportunity to play against some of the world's best male professional golfers at the Sony Open on the PGA Tour when the sponsor granted her an exemption. "It's like a dream come true," she said. For two months before the tournament, she practiced diligently in an effort to improve enough to make the cut at the Open. The event was being held on the tournament course near her home in Honolulu, so from November until the January tournament Wie played nearly 100 hours there. She spent her Thanksgiving school break at the David Leadbetter Academy in Orlando, Florida, learning to perfect her swing.

At the Sony Open in January 2004, Wie became the youngest player (and the fourth woman) to compete at a PGA event, giving her a chance to play with one of her heroes, Ernie Els, in a practice round. During the four-hour practice, Els taught Wie a new way to hit a long-range putt. Els advised her not to swing hard and smack the ball, but rather swing at the same pace through the entire stroke. After her practice round with Els, Wie said in a press conference that she was "very nervous" to play with him because "I didn't want to embarrass myself or anything. . . . I was more excited about this than the tournament." Praising Wie as a "phenomenal player," Els also said, "Michelle is 14. Give her a couple of years to get stronger. I mean, she can play on this tour. If she keeps working, keeps doing the right things, there's no reason why she shouldn't be out here."

————— " —————

Praising Wie as a "phenomenal player," Ernie Els once said, "Michelle is 14. Give her a couple of years to get stronger. I mean, she can play on this tour. If she keeps working, keeps doing the right things, there's no reason why she shouldn't be out here."

————— " —————

Wie's performance at the tournament impressed many golf fans. She hit the ball an average of 270 yards off the tee, five yards less than the average of all the players but 20 yards farther than her partner, professional Craig Bowden. She even impressed her caddy, Bobby Verwey, who said "That golf swing of hers, it's the best golf swing I've ever seen in my life." Wie's practice with Els showed in her putting; 13 of her holes were made with one putt. She made a total of eight putts longer than 40 feet, including one 60-footer and another 50-footer. In her second round, Wie became the first woman in history to shoot under-par at a men's PGA event, shooting a 68, or two under par. Although she made the course par of 140, the cut was 139. She missed it by one stroke. In the end, she had tied 16 other players for 80th place, including the British Open winner Ben Curtis and U.S. Open winner Jim Furyk, and finished ahead of 47 other professional male golfers. It was an outstanding performance for such a young teenager at a professional men's event.

Wie (left) and teammate Erica Blasberg celebrate their team's victory at the 2004 Curtis Cup Matches in Formby, England.

Recent Events

After her near-qualifying play at the Sony Open, invitations to other tournaments came pouring in. In March she finished in the Top 25 at her first LPGA event of the year, the Safeway International; she then finished fourth in the Kraft Nabisco Championship, her first LPGA major tournament of 2004.

In June 2004, Wie was the youngest player ever to be selected to represent the United States at the Curtis Cup Match in England. The Curtis Cup, which pits a team from the U.S. against a team from Great Britain and Ireland, has been played every other year since 1932. According to Wie, it was like being chosen to be in the Olympics. She and the seven other American players retained the U.S. dominance of the Curtis Cup for the fourth match in a row. Wie won both her singles matches to help the U.S. defeat Great Britain and Ireland 10-8. As an added reward, she accepted the 2004 World Newcomer of the Year Award at the Laureus World Sports Awards in Lisbon, Spain.

Wie continued her excellent play in the qualifier for the 2004 U.S. Amateur Public Links Championship, a men's event. She shot 71-71 and finished two strokes behind the winners. Although she failed to make the cut and earn a bid to the finals, she earned status by becoming one of the four alternates to the event. Soon after, she received an exemption from the sectional qualifying rounds of the U.S. Women's Open. The U.S. Golf Association executive director David Fay explained that based solely on her performance, Wie was offered the U.S. Women's Open second-ever exemption. The Open invites the top 35 professional players each year. Although she wasn't even a professional, Wie would have been ranked 28th if she had been a pro in 2004. The exemption was certainly an honor, but not undeserved. At the July 2004 event, she shot 71-70-71-73, tying for 13th place. At the age of 14, Wie had already made six holes-in-one—which is pretty impressive considering that some professionals have never made even one.

—— " ——

According to PGA veteran player Fred Couples, "When you see her hit a golf ball . . . there's nothing that prepares you for it. It's just the scariest thing you've ever seen."

—— " ——

Wie's Gifts as a Golfer

Wie has what many call "the gift," a kind of talent and charisma that can't be taught. Vice president of the PGA Tour Duke Butler said, "I honestly feel she's going to be one of the top 10 athletes of our lifetime." Many have said that Wie's powerful drive sets her apart from other female golfers. Her ability to send 300-yard drives with accuracy puts her in the same league as some of the top professional male golfers; her drives outdistance those by most female professional golfers by more than 50 yards. Her swing and strike have been described as "a dream," "perfect," and "unfathomable." According to PGA veteran player Fred Couples, "When you see her hit a golf ball . . . there's nothing that prepares you for it. It's just the scariest thing you've ever seen." Another player, fellow golfer Davis Love III, would agree. "She probably has one of the best golf swings I've ever seen, period," Love said. "She has a lot going for her. Plus, she's tall and strong. No telling what she's going to do when she gets a little older."

Wie has more than physical talent going for her. According to her father, "There is something unique, especially in her mind. . . . She can handle the pressure. She has something different." Her coach, Gary Gilchrist, echoes that idea. "She's got the touch, the feel, and the power," Gilchrist said. "All she needs is time. And she's got plenty of that." Wie has a kind of composure that few adults maintain in the heat of competition. Whether she's playing as the youngest among professional female golfers or as the only woman in a field of the game's best men, Wie remains cool and calm — even with thousands of fans crowding the course to catch a glimpse of her. "You kind of expect a 14-year-old to crack at this level," pro-golfer Kevin Hayashi said about playing with Wie on the PGA Tour.

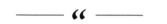

Fellow golfer Davis Love III said that "She probably has one of the best golf swings I've ever seen, period. She has a lot going for her. Plus, she's tall and strong. No telling what she's going to do when she gets a little older."

But Wie doesn't choke. She concentrates and tries her best. "Her poise is unbelievable," said *Golf Digest* writer Tom Lehman. "Either you've got it or you don't." Coach Gilchrist once admitted that "I'm expecting her, by the time she is 16, to have the mental capacity to play at any level. On any tour."

With all her natural talent comes a great deal of media attention. Her record-breaking firsts, her powerful shots, and, in her own words, her "freakishly tall" stature (she stands six-feet, one-inch tall), all draw journalists and cameras. Wie doesn't shy away from all the attention; in fact she thrives on it. "I always want to look at the tournaments where no one has gone in before, and I want to be the first one in everything," she said. Her father said that "Michelle really likes the media attention, she really likes the fans. She signs autographs with a smile."

Is Wie's Youth Being Stolen?

Wie's penchant for playing against professionals — rather than other amateurs closer to her age — has inspired some concerns in the golf world. Some observers wonder if she is being pushed too hard by her parents and if she is trying to do too much, too soon. But her supporters disagree. "It's her ambition," her mentor Yao said. "All [her parents are] doing is encouraging and supporting it." Her coach Gary Gilchrist said that Wie and her family do a good job of balancing her life. "[When] I first met them, I could tell Michelle loves school in Hawaii. She has great friends in Hawaii, and her mom and dad had done a great job with her game. I could tell there

Wie tees off at the 2004 U.S. Women's Open, where she posted the best score of all amateur players, nine shots behind winner Meg Mallon.

was a great balance." Many believe that her parents are not pushing her to turn pro or to make money; instead, they have said that she will remain an amateur for several more years, until she is an adult.

Wie does well in school, enjoys her friends, relaxes in front of the Disney Channel, and plays golf. Her schedule includes a 30-minute workout of her core muscles each day, three hours of golf after each school day, and eight hours every weekend. But Wie doesn't think of the time as drudgery; she's having fun. "I just like everything about golf, really," Wie admitted.

Other observers trying to assess her emotional and social development have called her intelligent, charming, well-adjusted, happy, and very ma-

153

ture. They claim that she seems to socialize easily with peers and with adults, and also seems to get along well with her parents.

Future Path

Wie's performance on the golf course at such a young age makes some analysts worry about her future. Will she be exploited by sponsors hoping to entice the public and to draw attention to the sport? Confronting that issue will be tough for the Wies. The family has few role models to follow, since few young people have demonstrated such great talent so early in life.

Tiger Woods might be the best example, but he took a very different path. His father, Earl Woods, wanted his son to learn how to win before turning pro. He concentrated his son's efforts on dominating junior tournaments, preventing him from playing professionals until he turned 16. The Wies have a different approach. Michelle has been playing in professional tournaments since age 10, but she hasn't won many tournaments. The Wies' strategy is to offer their daughter the chance to play with and learn from the world's best golfers. After Michelle played a practice round with Ernie Els at the Sony Open, her father said that "Michelle is a visual learner, and that's the beauty of her entering PGA Tour events. Because you can learn so much from a player like that."

> *According to her father, "There is something unique, especially in her mind. . . . She can handle the pressure. She has something different."*

Wie's schedule for the coming years will most likely be a mix of junior and professional tournaments. Eventually, she plans to split her time between women's and men's tournaments, hoping at some point to beat Tiger Woods in competition. "It's like my hobby, playing in men's tournaments, because they're really exciting and give me something new to try. I want to go to the next level. I don't want to restrict myself to one level," Wie once said. Her ultimate dream is to play the Masters at Augusta National some day, which no woman has ever done. "I'm not looking to prove a point," Wie explained. "I just want to play the best there is." As an amateur Wie can qualify to play at the Masters if she wins the U.S. Amateur, the U.S. Mid-Amateur, or the U.S. Public Links men's tournaments. Talking about women playing against men in the future, Wie said that "I don't think it will be such a big deal later on. Women will want to go farther. More women will be brave enough to play against the men."

Wie with her father, B.J. Wie, who has often served as her caddy.

Golf fans are watching Wie with great anticipation, eager to see what the future will bring. As Bob Williams of Burns Sports Celebrity Service explained, "she has the ability to forever change the attitudes and opinions of people in sport." When asked how she sees the future, Wie confided that "I guess I'm not normal first of all, so I can't have a normal life. I guess if you grow up normal, you'll always be normal, and I don't want to be normal. I want to be something else."

EDUCATION

Wie attends Punahour High School near her home in Hawaii. She stays focused by separating her life into neat compartments: "When I'm in school, I don't even want to think about golf. It's just school and my friends," she once said. "When I'm on the golf course, I don't really feel like a ninth-grader." Wie is so attached to her home and friends that she turned down a full scholarship to one of the country's top golf schools, the David Leadbetter Academy.

> **"She's got the touch, the feel, and the power," said her coach, Gary Gilchrist. "All she needs is time. And she's got plenty of that."**

Wie, a mostly A-student, is already thinking about college. She is looking at Stanford—the alma mater of her uncle as well as her hero Tiger Woods, and the school where her grandfather taught as a visiting professor from Korea. "I want to be an educated person," Wie has said. When asked whether she's tempted to become a professional golfer soon so that she can start winning lots of money, she replied that first, "I'd like to go through the basic steps of life, like go to high school and then go to college and be in a dorm and stuff like that. I think I just want to go through the basic steps of life, and then I think I'd be fine from then."

Certainly Wie's attitudes about her life have been influenced by her parents. Both tour with her regularly, and until recently her father served as her caddy. Her parents, with whom she speaks Korean, are very careful to balance their daughter's golfing life with good doses of friends and school. "There's a very fine line between challenging and pushing," 19-year-old golf prodigy Christina Kim said, adding "She's not being pushed at all."

FAVORITE FOOD

Wie's favorite food is a Korean stew called Kimchee Chigae and rice.

MAJOR INFLUENCES

Wie often lists Ernie Els and Tiger Woods as her golf heroes. Wie has said that she tried to copy their golf swings, first imitating Woods and then Els. She is a good study; her smooth, effortless swing has earned her the nickname "The Big Wiesy," a takeoff on Els's nickname "The Big Easy."

HOBBIES AND OTHER INTERESTS

Wie has said that she ranks shopping as one of her favorite things to do. She likes to go to the mall with her friends, and she also likes to read, draw, watch television, use the computer, and listen to Coldplay and Good Charlotte.

HONORS AND AWARDS

Hawaii State Women's Stroke Play Championship: 2001
Jennie K. Wilson Invitational, Hawaii: 2001
Hawaii State Open: 2002, Women's Division Winner
U.S. Women's Amateur Public Links Championship: 2003

FURTHER READING

Periodicals

Detroit News, Aug. 13, 2003, p.E1
Golf World, June 27, 2003, p.18; Jan. 23, 2004, p.14
Honolulu Advertiser, Mar. 20, 2003, p.D6; June 8, 2003, p.C1; Sep. 16, 2003, p.D1; Nov. 9, 2003, p.C1
Houston Chronicle, July 2, 2003, p.1
Los Angeles Times, Jan. 13, 2004, p.D1; Jan.14, 2004, p.D1; Mar. 25, 2004, p.D3; Mar. 27, 2004, p.D6
New York Times, Jan. 13, 2004, p.D1; Mar. 29, 2004, p.D3
Orlando Sentinel, June 25, 2003, p.D8
Palm Beach Post, June 29, 2003, p.B1
Sports Illustrated, July 7, 2003, p.32; July 14, 2003, p.G6; Jan. 26, 2004, p.17; May 3, 2004
Sports Illustrated for Kids, Aug. 1, 2003, p.47
USA Today, June 27, 2003, p.C1; Mar. 24, 2004, Sports section

Online Articles

http://sports.espn.go.com/golf/news/story?id=1832101
    (*ESPN,* "Girl on the Verge," June 19, 3004)

http://www.golfdigest.com/gfw/gfwinstruction/index.ssf?/gfw
/gfwinstruction/gfw200310wie.html
(*Golf Digest*, "Michelle Wie Steps Up," Sep.-Oct. 2003)
http://www.golfdigest.com/features/index.ssf?/features/gd200408myshot
.html
(*Golf Digest*, "My Shot: Michelle Wie," Aug. 2004)
http://www.kidzworld.com/site/p1848.htm
(*KidzWorld*, "Michelle Wie: Pro Golfer," no date)
http://www.lpga.com/entertainment_content.aspx?pid=2483&mid=3
(*LPGA*, "Quick 18 with Amateur Michelle Wie," no date)

Other

"60 Minutes" TV transcript, CBS News, Apr. 11, 2004

ADDRESS

Michelle Wie
LPGA
100 International Golf Drive
Daytona Beach, FL 32124

WORLD WIDE WEB SITE

http://sports.espn.go.com/golf/players

Photo and Illustration Credits

Francie Berger/Photos: copyright © Nancy Rica Schiff from her book, *Odd Jobs: Portraits of Unusual Occupations* (pp. 9, 16) ; AP/Wide World Photos (pp. 12, 15).

Orlando Bloom/Photos: Kevin Winter/Getty Images; copyright © 2001 New Line Productions, Inc. (p. 26); copyright © 2002 New Line Productions, Inc.(p. 29); Elliott Marks, SMPSP/copyright © Disney Enterprises, Inc. and Jerry Bruckheimer, Inc. All rights reserved (p. 31); Sidney Baldwin/copyright © 2001 Revolution Studios (bottom, p. 31); Alex Bailey/copyright © 2004 Warner Bros. Entertainment Inc. (p.33); Matt Dunham/Reuters (p.35).

Carla Hayden/Photos: ALA; Enoch Pratt Free Library (pp. 41, 43); AP/Wide World Photos; Hilary Schwab.

Lindsay Lohan/Photos: Jim Ruymen/Reuters; Lorey Sebastian/copyright © Disney Enterprises, Inc. All rights reserved; copyright © Disney; Ron Batzdorff/copyright © Disney Enterprises, Inc. All rights reserved; Michael Gibson/tm & copyright © 2004 Paramount Pictures; Mark Mainz/Getty Images. DVD cover: copyright © Buena Vista Home Entertainment. Cover: tm & copyright © 2004 Paramount Pictures.

OutKast/Photos: Jason Szenes/EPA/Landov; copyright © John Halpern/Retna; Frank Micelotta/Getty Images; Kevin Winter/Getty Images; AP/Wide World Photos. CD covers: SOUTHERNPLAYALISTICADILLACMUZIK (p) 1993,1994 & copyright © LaFace Records; SPEAKERBOXX/THE LOVE BELOW (p) & copyright © 2003 Arista Records, Inc.; STANKONIA (p) & copyright © 2000 Arista Records, Inc. Cover: Albert Ferreira/Reuters/Landov.

Ronald Reagan/Photos: courtesy Ronald Reagan Library (pp. 83, 85, 88, 91, 98, 100, 102, 105, 106, 108); AP/Wide World Photos (pp. 93, 94, 97).

Ricardo Sanchez/Photos: Mike Theiler/EPA/Landov; Scott Nelson/Getty Images; PFC Joshua Hutcheson/photo courtesy of U.S. Army; USDOD; Jamal A. Wilson/EPA/Landov; Chris Hondros/Getty Images.

Brian Urlacher/Photos: Brian Bahr/Getty Images; Marc Piscotty/Getty Images; Frank Polich/UPI/Landov; Gary Cameron/Reuters/Landov; Sue Ogrocki/Reuters; AP/Wide World Photos.

Michelle Wie/Photos: Stuart Franklin/Getty Images; Jonathan Ferrey/Getty Images; Kim Kyung-Hoon/Reuters/Landov; Stuart Franklin/Getty Images; Andy Lyons/Getty Images; AP/Wide World Photos.

How to Use the Cumulative Index

Our indexes have a new look. In an effort to make our indexes easier to use, we've combined the Name and General Index into a new, Cumulative Index. This single ready-reference resource covers all the volumes in *Biography Today*, both the general series and the special subject series. The new Cumulative Index contains complete listings of all individuals who have appeared in *Biography Today* since the series began. Their names appear in bold-faced type, followed by the issue in which they appear. The Cumulative Index also includes references for the occupations, nationalities, and ethnic and minority origins of individuals profiled in *Biography Today*.

We have also made some changes to our specialty indexes, the Places of Birth Index and the Birthday Index. To consolidate and to save space, the Places of Birth Index and the Birthday Index will no longer appear in the January and April issues of the softbound subscription series. But these indexes can still be found in the September issue of the softbound subscription series, in the hardbound Annual Cumulation at the end of each year, and in each volume of the special subject series.

General Series

The General Series of *Biography Today* is denoted in the index with the month and year of the issue in which the individual appeared. Each individual also appears in the Annual Cumulation for that year.

Special Subject Series

The Special Subject Series of *Biography Today* are each denoted in the index with an abbreviated form of the series name, plus the number of the volume in which the individual appears. They are listed as follows.

Adams, Ansel . . . . Artist V.1	(Artists)
Bloor, Edward . . . . Author V.15	(Authors)
Diaz, Cameron . . . . PerfArt V.3	(Performing Artists)
Fay, Michael . . . . Science V.9	(Scientists & Inventors)
McGrady, Tracy . . . . Sport V.11	(Sports)
Peterson, Roger Tory . . . . WorLdr V.1	(World Leaders: Environmental Leaders)
Sadat, Anwar . . . . WorLdr V.2	(World Leaders: Modern African Leaders)
Wolf, Hazel. . . . . WorLdr V.3	(World Leaders: Environmental Leaders 2)

Updates

Updated information on selected individuals appears in the Appendix at the end of some issues of the *Biography Today* Annual Cumulation. In the index, the original entry is listed first, followed by any updates.

Arafat, Yasir . . . . Sep 94; Update 94;
Update 95; Update 96; Update 97; Update 98;
Update 00; Update 01; Update 02
Gates, Bill . . . . Apr 93; Update 98;
Update 00; Science V.5; Update 01
Griffith Joyner, Florence. . . . . Sport V.1;
Update 98
Sanders, Barry . . . . Sep 95; Update 99
Spock, Dr. Benjamin . . . . Sep 95; Update 98
Yeltsin, Boris . . . . Apr 92; Update 93;
Update 95; Update 96; Update 98; Update 00

Cumulative Index

This cumulative index includes names, occupations, nationalities, and ethnic and minority origins that pertain to all individuals profiled in *Biography Today* since the debut of the series in 1992.

191

Places of Birth Index

The following index lists the places of birth for the individuals profiled in *Biography Today*. Places of birth are entered under state, province, and/or country.

PLACES OF BIRTH INDEX

Birthday Index

BIRTHDAY INDEX

Biography Today

General Series

For ages 9 and above

B iography Today **General Series** includes a unique combination of current biographical profiles that teachers and librarians — and the readers themselves — tell us are most appealing. The **General Series** is available as a 3-issue subscription; hardcover annual cumulation; or subscription plus cumulation.

Within the **General Series**, your readers will find a variety of sketches about:

- Authors
- Musicians
- Political leaders
- Sports figures
- Movie actresses & actors
- Cartoonists
- Scientists
- Astronauts
- TV personalities
- and the movers & shakers in many other fields!

"*Biography Today* will be useful in elementary and middle school libraries and in public library children's collections where there is a need for biographies of current personalities. High schools serving reluctant readers may also want to consider a subscription."

— *Booklist,* American Library Association

"Highly recommended for the young adult audience. Readers will delight in the accessible, energetic, tell-all style; teachers, librarians, and parents will welcome the clever format, intelligent and informative text. It should prove especially useful in motivating 'reluctant' readers or literate nonreaders."

— *MultiCultural Review*

"Written in a friendly, almost chatty tone, the profiles offer quick, objective information. While coverage of current figures makes *Biography Today* a useful reference tool, an appealing format and wide scope make it a fun resource to browse." — *School Library Journal*

"The best source for current information at a level kids can understand."

— Kelly Bryant, School Librarian, Carlton, OR

"Easy for kids to read. We love it! Don't want to be without it."

— Lynn McWhirter, School Librarian, Rockford, IL

ONE-YEAR SUBSCRIPTION

- 3 softcover issues, 6" x 9"
- Published in January, April, and September
- 1-year subscription, $60
- 150 pages per issue
- 10 profiles per issue
- Contact sources for additional information
- Cumulative General, Places of Birth, and Birthday Indexes

HARDBOUND ANNUAL CUMULATION

- Sturdy 6" x 9" hardbound volume
- Published in December
- $62 per volume
- 450 pages per volume
- 25-30 profiles — includes all profiles found in softcover issues for that calendar year
- Cumulative General, Places of Birth, and Birthday Indexes
- Special appendix features current updates of previous profiles

SUBSCRIPTION AND CUMULATION COMBINATION

- $99 for 3 softcover issues plus the hardbound volume

1992

Paula Abdul
Andre Agassi
Kirstie Alley
Terry Anderson
Roseanne Arnold
Isaac Asimov
James Baker
Charles Barkley
Larry Bird
Judy Blume
Berke Breathed
Garth Brooks
Barbara Bush
George Bush
Fidel Castro
Bill Clinton
Bill Cosby
Diana, Princess of Wales
Shannen Doherty
Elizabeth Dole
David Duke
Gloria Estefan
Mikhail Gorbachev
Steffi Graf
Wayne Gretzky
Matt Groening
Alex Haley
Hammer
Martin Handford
Stephen Hawking
Hulk Hogan
Saddam Hussein
Lee Iacocca
Bo Jackson
Mae Jemison
Peter Jennings
Steven Jobs
Pope John Paul II
Magic Johnson
Michael Jordon
Jackie Joyner-Kersee
Spike Lee
Mario Lemieux
Madeleine L'Engle
Jay Leno
Yo-Yo Ma
Nelson Mandela
Wynton Marsalis
Thurgood Marshall
Ann Martin
Barbara McClintock
Emily Arnold McCully
Antonia Novello

Sandra Day O'Connor
Rosa Parks
Jane Pauley
H. Ross Perot
Luke Perry
Scottie Pippen
Colin Powell
Jason Priestley
Queen Latifah
Yitzhak Rabin
Sally Ride
Pete Rose
Nolan Ryan
H. Norman
    Schwarzkopf
Jerry Seinfeld
Dr. Seuss
Gloria Steinem
Clarence Thomas
Chris Van Allsburg
Cynthia Voigt
Bill Watterson
Robin Williams
Oprah Winfrey
Kristi Yamaguchi
Boris Yeltsin

1993

Maya Angelou
Arthur Ashe
Avi
Kathleen Battle
Candice Bergen
Boutros Boutros-Ghali
Chris Burke
Dana Carvey
Cesar Chavez
Henry Cisneros
Hillary Rodham Clinton
Jacques Cousteau
Cindy Crawford
Macaulay Culkin
Lois Duncan
Marian Wright Edelman
Cecil Fielder
Bill Gates
Sara Gilbert
Dizzy Gillespie
Al Gore
Cathy Guisewite
Jasmine Guy
Anita Hill
Ice-T
Darci Kistler

k.d. lang
Dan Marino
Rigoberta Menchu
Walter Dean Myers
Martina Navratilova
Phyllis Reynolds Naylor
Rudolf Nureyev
Shaquille O'Neal
Janet Reno
Jerry Rice
Mary Robinson
Winona Ryder
Jerry Spinelli
Denzel Washington
Keenen Ivory Wayans
Dave Winfield

1994

Tim Allen
Marian Anderson
Mario Andretti
Ned Andrews
Yasir Arafat
Bruce Babbitt
Mayim Bialik
Bonnie Blair
Ed Bradley
John Candy
Mary Chapin Carpenter
Benjamin Chavis
Connie Chung
Beverly Cleary
Kurt Cobain
F.W. de Klerk
Rita Dove
Linda Ellerbee
Sergei Fedorov
Zlata Filipovic
Daisy Fuentes
Ruth Bader Ginsburg
Whoopi Goldberg
Tonya Harding
Melissa Joan Hart
Geoff Hooper
Whitney Houston
Dan Jansen
Nancy Kerrigan
Alexi Lalas
Charlotte Lopez
Wilma Mankiller
Shannon Miller
Toni Morrison
Richard Nixon
Greg Norman
Severo Ochoa

River Phoenix
Elizabeth Pine
Jonas Salk
Richard Scarry
Emmitt Smith
Will Smith
Steven Spielberg
Patrick Stewart
R.L. Stine
Lewis Thomas
Barbara Walters
Charlie Ward
Steve Young
Kim Zmeskal

1995

Troy Aikman
Jean-Bertrand Aristide
Oksana Baiul
Halle Berry
Benazir Bhutto
Jonathan Brandis
Warren E. Burger
Ken Burns
Candace Cameron
Jimmy Carter
Agnes de Mille
Placido Domingo
Janet Evans
Patrick Ewing
Newt Gingrich
John Goodman
Amy Grant
Jesse Jackson
James Earl Jones
Julie Krone
David Letterman
Rush Limbaugh
Heather Locklear
Reba McEntire
Joe Montana
Cosmas Ndeti
Hakeem Olajuwon
Ashley Olsen
Mary-Kate Olsen
Jennifer Parkinson
Linus Pauling
Itzhak Perlman
Cokie Roberts
Wilma Rudolph
Salt 'N' Pepa
Barry Sanders
William Shatner
Elizabeth George
    Speare

Dr. Benjamin Spock
Jonathan Taylor
    Thomas
Vicki Van Meter
Heather Whitestone
Pedro Zamora

1996

Aung San Suu Kyi
Boyz II Men
Brandy
Ron Brown
Mariah Carey
Jim Carrey
Larry Champagne III
Christo
Chelsea Clinton
Coolio
Bob Dole
David Duchovny
Debbi Fields
Chris Galeczka
Jerry Garcia
Jennie Garth
Wendy Guey
Tom Hanks
Alison Hargreaves
Sir Edmund Hillary
Judith Jamison
Barbara Jordan
Annie Leibovitz
Carl Lewis
Jim Lovell
Mickey Mantle
Lynn Margulis
Iqbal Masih
Mark Messier
Larisa Oleynik
Christopher Pike
David Robinson
Dennis Rodman
Selena
Monica Seles
Don Shula
Kerri Strug
Tiffani-Amber Thiessen
Dave Thomas
Jaleel White

1997

Madeleine Albright
Marcus Allen
Gillian Anderson
Rachel Blanchard
Zachery Ty Bryan
Adam Ezra Cohen
Claire Danes
Celine Dion
Jean Driscoll
Louis Farrakhan
Ella Fitzgerald
Harrison Ford
Bryant Gumbel
John Johnson
Michael Johnson
Maya Lin
George Lucas
John Madden
Bill Monroe
Alanis Morissette
Sam Morrison
Rosie O'Donnell
Muammar el-Qaddafi
Christopher Reeve
Pete Sampras
Pat Schroeder
Rebecca Sealfon
Tupac Shakur
Tabitha Soren
Herbert Tarvin
Merlin Tuttle
Mara Wilson

1998

Bella Abzug
Kofi Annan
Neve Campbell
Sean Combs (Puff
    Daddy)
Dalai Lama (Tenzin
    Gyatso)
Diana, Princess of Wales
Leonardo DiCaprio
Walter E. Diemer
Ruth Handler
Hanson
Livan Hernandez
Jewel
Jimmy Johnson
Tara Lipinski
Jody-Anne Maxwell
Dominique Moceanu
Alexandra Nechita

Brad Pitt
LeAnn Rimes
Emily Rosa
David Satcher
Betty Shabazz
Kordell Stewart
Shinichi Suzuki
Mother Teresa
Mike Vernon
Reggie White
Kate Winslet

1999

Ben Affleck
Jennifer Aniston
Maurice Ashley
Kobe Bryant
Bessie Delany
Sadie Delany
Sharon Draper
Sarah Michelle Gellar
John Glenn
Savion Glover
Jeff Gordon
David Hampton
Lauryn Hill
King Hussein
Lynn Johnston
Shari Lewis
Oseola McCarty
Mark McGwire
Slobodan Milosevic
Natalie Portman
J. K. Rowling
Frank Sinatra
Gene Siskel
Sammy Sosa
John Stanford
Natalia Toro
Shania Twain
Mitsuko Uchida
Jesse Ventura
Venus Williams

2000

Christina Aguilera
K.A. Applegate
Lance Armstrong
Backstreet Boys
Daisy Bates
Harry Blackmun
George W. Bush
Carson Daly
Ron Dayne
Henry Louis Gates, Jr.
Doris Haddock
    (Granny D)
Jennifer Love Hewitt
Chamique Holdsclaw
Katie Holmes
Charlayne Hunter-Gault
Johanna Johnson
Craig Kielburger
John Lasseter
Peyton Manning
Ricky Martin
John McCain
Walter Payton
Freddie Prinze, Jr.
Viviana Risca
Briana Scurry
George Thampy
CeCe Winans

2001

Jessica Alba
Christiane Amanpour
Drew Barrymore
Jeff Bezos
Destiny's Child
Dale Earnhardt
Carly Fiorina
Aretha Franklin
Cathy Freeman
Tony Hawk
Faith Hill
Kim Dae-jung
Madeleine L'Engle
Mariangela Lisanti
Frankie Muniz
*N Sync
Ellen Ochoa
Jeff Probst
Julia Roberts
Carl T. Rowan
Britney Spears
Chris Tucker
Lloyd D. Ward
Alan Webb
Chris Weinke

2002

Aaliyah
Osama bin Laden
Mary J. Blige
Aubyn Burnside
Aaron Carter
Julz Chavez
Dick Cheney
Hilary Duff
Billy Gilman
Rudolph Giuliani
Brian Griese
Jennifer Lopez
Dave Mirra
Dineh Mohajer
Leanne Nakamura
Daniel Radcliffe
Condoleezza Rice
Marla Runyan
Ruth Simmons
Mattie Stepanek
J.R.R. Tolkien
Barry Watson
Tyrone Willingham
Elijah Wood

2003

Yolanda Adams
Olivia Bennett
Mildred Benson
Alexis Bledel
Barry Bonds
Vincent Brooks
Laura Bush
Amanda Bynes
Kelly Clarkson
Vin Diesel
Eminem
Michele Forman
Vicente Fox
Millard Fuller
Josh Hartnett
Dolores Huerta

Sarah Hughes
Enrique Iglesias
Jeanette Lee
John Lewis
Nicklas Lidstrom
Clint Mathis
Donovan McNabb
Nelly
Andy Roddick
Gwen Stefani
Emma Watson
Meg Whitman
Reese Witherspoon
Yao Ming

2004

Natalie Babbitt
David Beckham
Francie Berger
Tony Blair
Orlando Bloom
Kim Clijsters
Celia Cruz
Matel Dawson, Jr.
The Donnas
Tim Duncan
Shirin Ebadi
Carla Hayden
Ashton Kutcher
Lisa Leslie
Linkin Park
Lindsay Lohan
Irene D. Long
John Mayer
Mandy Moore
Thich Nhat Hanh
OutKast
Raven
Ronald Reagan
Keanu Reeves
Ricardo Sanchez
Brian Urlacher
Alexa Vega
Michelle Wie
Will Wright

Biography Today

Subject Series

Expands and complements the General Series and targets specific subject areas . . .

Our readers asked for it! They wanted more biographies, and the *Biography Today* **Subject Series** is our response to that demand. Now your readers can choose their special areas of interest and go on to read about their favorites in those fields. Priced at just $39 per volume, the following specific volumes are included in the *Biography Today* **Subject Series:**

- **Artists**
- **Authors**
- **Performing Artists**
- **Scientists & Inventors**
- **Sports**
- **World Leaders**
  Environmental Leaders
  Modern African Leaders

FEATURES AND FORMAT

- Sturdy 6" x 9" hardbound volumes
- Individual volumes, $39 each
- 200 pages per volume
- 10 profiles per volume — targets individuals within a specific subject area
- Contact sources for additional information
- Cumulative General, Places of Birth, and Birthday Indexes

NOTE: There is *no duplication of entries* between the **General Series** of *Biography Today* and the **Subject Series.**

AUTHORS

"A useful tool for children's assignment needs." — *School Library Journal*

"The prose is workmanlike: report writers will find enough detail to begin sound investigations, and browsers are likely to find someone of interest." — *School Library Journal*

SCIENTISTS & INVENTORS

"The articles are readable, attractively laid out, and touch on important points that will suit assignment needs. Browsers will note the clear writing and interesting details."
— *School Library Journal*

"The book is excellent for demonstrating that scientists are real people with widely diverse backgrounds and personal interests. The biographies are fascinating to read."
— *The Science Teacher*

SPORTS

"This series should become a standard resource in libraries that serve intermediate students." — *School Library Journal*

ENVIRONMENTAL LEADERS #1

"A tremendous book that fills a gap in the biographical category of books. This is a great reference book." — *Science Scope*

Artists

VOLUME 1

Ansel Adams
Romare Bearden
Margaret Bourke-White
Alexander Calder
Marc Chagall
Helen Frankenthaler
Jasper Johns
Jacob Lawrence
Henry Moore
Grandma Moses
Louise Nevelson
Georgia O'Keeffe
Gordon Parks
I.M. Pei
Diego Rivera
Norman Rockwell
Andy Warhol
Frank Lloyd Wright

Authors

VOLUME 1

Eric Carle
Alice Childress
Robert Cormier
Roald Dahl
Jim Davis
John Grisham
Virginia Hamilton
James Herriot
S.E. Hinton
M.E. Kerr
Stephen King
Gary Larson
Joan Lowery Nixon
Gary Paulsen
Cynthia Rylant
Mildred D. Taylor
Kurt Vonnegut, Jr.
E.B. White
Paul Zindel

VOLUME 2

James Baldwin
Stan and Jan Berenstain
David Macaulay
Patricia MacLachlan
Scott O'Dell
Jerry Pinkney
Jack Prelutsky

Lynn Reid Banks
Faith Ringgold
J.D. Salinger
Charles Schulz
Maurice Sendak
P.L. Travers
Garth Williams

VOLUME 3

Candy Dawson Boyd
Ray Bradbury
Gwendolyn Brooks
Ralph W. Ellison
Louise Fitzhugh
Jean Craighead George
E.L. Konigsburg
C.S. Lewis
Fredrick L. McKissack
Patricia C. McKissack
Katherine Paterson
Anne Rice
Shel Silverstein
Laura Ingalls Wilder

VOLUME 4

Betsy Byars
Chris Carter
Caroline B. Cooney
Christopher Paul Curtis
Anne Frank
Robert Heinlein
Marguerite Henry
Lois Lowry
Melissa Mathison
Bill Peet
August Wilson

VOLUME 5

Sharon Creech
Michael Crichton
Karen Cushman
Tomie dePaola
Lorraine Hansberry
Karen Hesse
Brian Jacques
Gary Soto
Richard Wright
Laurence Yep

VOLUME 6

Lloyd Alexander
Paula Danziger
Nancy Farmer
Zora Neale Hurston

Shirley Jackson
Angela Johnson
Jon Krakauer
Leo Lionni
Francine Pascal
Louis Sachar
Kevin Williamson

VOLUME 7

William H. Armstrong
Patricia Reilly Giff
Langston Hughes
Stan Lee
Julius Lester
Robert Pinsky
Todd Strasser
Jacqueline Woodson
Patricia C. Wrede
Jane Yolen

VOLUME 8

Amelia Atwater-Rhodes
Barbara Cooney
Paul Laurence Dunbar
Ursula K. Le Guin
Farley Mowat
Naomi Shihab Nye
Daniel Pinkwater
Beatrix Potter
Ann Rinaldi

VOLUME 9

Robb Armstrong
Cherie Bennett
Bruce Coville
Rosa Guy
Harper Lee
Irene Gut Opdyke
Philip Pullman
Jon Scieszka
Amy Tan
Joss Whedon

VOLUME 10

David Almond
Joan Bauer
Kate DiCamillo
Jack Gantos
Aaron McGruder
Richard Peck
Andrea Davis Pinkney
Louise Rennison
David Small
Katie Tarbox

VOLUME 11

Laurie Halse Anderson
Bryan Collier
Margaret Peterson
   Haddix
Milton Meltzer
William Sleator
Sonya Sones
Genndy Tartakovsky
Wendelin Van Draanen
Ruth White

VOLUME 12

An Na
Claude Brown
Meg Cabot
Virginia Hamilton
Chuck Jones
Robert Lipsyte
Lillian Morrison
Linda Sue Park
Pam Muñoz Ryan
Lemony Snicket
   (Daniel Handler)

VOLUME 13

Andrew Clements
Eoin Colfer
Sharon Flake
Edward Gorey
Francisco Jiménez
Astrid Lindgren
Chris Lynch
Marilyn Nelson
Tamora Pierce
Virginia Euwer Wolff

VOLUME 14

Orson Scott Card
Russell Freedman
Mary GrandPré
Dan Greenburg
Nikki Grimes
Laura Hillenbrand
Stephen Hillenburg
Norton Juster
Lurlene McDaniel
Stephanie S. Tolan

VOLUME 15

Liv Arnesen
Edward Bloor
Ann Brashares
Veronica Chambers
Mark Crilley
Paula Fox
Diana Wynne Jones
Victor Martinez
Robert McCloskey
Jerry Scott and Jim
  Borgman

Performing Artists

VOLUME 1

Jackie Chan
Dixie Chicks
Kirsten Dunst
Suzanne Farrell
Bernie Mac
Shakira
Isaac Stern
Julie Taymor
Usher
Christina Vidal

VOLUME 2

Ashanti
Tyra Banks
Peter Jackson
Norah Jones
Quincy Jones
Avril Lavigne
George López
Marcel Marceau
Eddie Murphy
Julia Stiles

VOLUME 3

Michelle Branch
Cameron Diaz
Missy Elliott
Evelyn Glennie
Benji Madden
Joel Madden
Mike Myers
Fred Rogers
Twyla Tharp
Tom Welling
Yuen Wo-Ping

Scientists & Inventors

VOLUME 1

John Bardeen
Sylvia Earle
Dian Fossey
Jane Goodall
Bernadine Healy
Jack Horner
Mathilde Krim
Edwin Land
Louise & Mary Leakey
Rita Levi-Montalcini
J. Robert Oppenheimer
Albert Sabin
Carl Sagan
James D. Watson

VOLUME 2

Jane Brody
Seymour Cray
Paul Erdös
Walter Gilbert
Stephen Jay Gould
Shirley Ann Jackson
Raymond Kurzweil
Shannon Lucid
Margaret Mead
Garrett Morgan
Bill Nye
Eloy Rodriguez
An Wang

VOLUME 3

Luis W. Alvarez
Hans A. Bethe
Gro Harlem Brundtland
Mary S. Calderone
Ioana Dumitriu
Temple Grandin
John Langston
  Gwaltney
Bernard Harris
Jerome Lemelson
Susan Love
Ruth Patrick
Oliver Sacks
Richie Stachowski

VOLUME 4

David Attenborough
Robert Ballard
Ben Carson

Eileen Collins
Biruté Galdikas
Lonnie Johnson
Meg Lowman
Forrest Mars Sr.
Akio Morita
Janese Swanson

VOLUME 5

Steve Case
Douglas Engelbart
Shawn Fanning
Sarah Flannery
Bill Gates
Laura Groppe
Grace Murray Hopper
Steven Jobs
Rand and Robyn Miller
Shigeru Miyamoto
Steve Wozniak

VOLUME 6

Hazel Barton
Alexa Canady
Arthur Caplan
Francis Collins
Gertrude Elion
Henry Heimlich
David Ho
Kenneth Kamler
Lucy Spelman
Lydia Villa-Komaroff

VOLUME 7

Tim Berners-Lee
France Córdova
Anthony S. Fauci
Sue Hendrickson
Steve Irwin
John Forbes Nash, Jr.
Jerri Nielsen
Ryan Patterson
Nina Vasan
Gloria WilderBrathwaite

VOLUME 8

Deborah Blum
Richard Carmona
Helene Gayle
Dave Kapell
Adriana C. Ocampo
John Romero
Jamie Rubin
Jill Tarter
Earl Warrick
Edward O. Wilson

VOLUME 9

Robert Barron
Regina Benjamin
Jim Cantore
Marion Donovan
Michael Fay
Laura L. Kiessling
Alvin Poussaint
Sandra Steingraber
Edward Teller
Peggy Whitson

Sports

VOLUME 1

Hank Aaron
Kareem Abdul-Jabbar
Hassiba Boulmerka
Susan Butcher
Beth Daniel
Chris Evert
Ken Griffey, Jr.
Florence Griffith Joyner
Grant Hill
Greg LeMond
Pelé
Uta Pippig
Cal Ripken, Jr.
Arantxa Sanchez
  Vicario
Deion Sanders
Tiger Woods

VOLUME 2

Muhammad Ali
Donovan Bailey
Gail Devers
John Elway
Brett Favre
Mia Hamm
Anfernee "Penny"
  Hardaway
Martina Hingis
Gordie Howe
Jack Nicklaus
Richard Petty
Dot Richardson
Sheryl Swoopes
Steve Yzerman

VOLUME 3

Joe Dumars
Jim Harbaugh
Dominik Hasek
Michelle Kwan
Rebecca Lobo
Greg Maddux
Fatuma Roba
Jackie Robinson
John Stockton
Picabo Street
Pat Summitt
Amy Van Dyken

VOLUME 4

Wilt Chamberlain
Brandi Chastain
Derek Jeter
Karch Kiraly
Alex Lowe
Randy Moss
Se Ri Pak
Dawn Riley
Karen Smyers
Kurt Warner
Serena Williams

VOLUME 5

Vince Carter
Lindsay Davenport
Lisa Fernandez
Fu Mingxia
Jaromir Jagr
Marion Jones
Pedro Martinez
Warren Sapp
Jenny Thompson
Karrie Webb

VOLUME 6

Jennifer Capriati
Stacy Dragila
Kevin Garnett
Eddie George
Alex Rodriguez
Joe Sakic
Annika Sorenstam
Jackie Stiles
Tiger Woods
Aliy Zirkle

VOLUME 7

Tom Brady
Tara Dakides
Alison Dunlap

Sergio Garcia
Allen Iverson
Shirley Muldowney
Ty Murray
Patrick Roy
Tasha Schwiker

VOLUME 8

Simon Ammann
Shannon Bahrke
Kelly Clark
Vonetta Flowers
Cammi Granato
Chris Klug
Jonny Moseley
Apolo Ohno
Sylke Otto
Ryne Sanborn
Jim Shea, Jr.

VOLUME 9

Tori Allen
Layne Beachley
Sue Bird
Fabiola da Silva
Randy Johnson
Jason Kidd
Tony Stewart
Michael Vick
Ted Williams
Jay Yelas

VOLUME 10

Ryan Boyle
Natalie Coughlin
Allyson Felix
Dallas Friday
Jean-Sébastien Giguère
Phil Jackson
Keyshawn Johnson
Tiffeny Milbrett
Alfonso Soriano
Diana Taurasi

VOLUME 11

Laila Ali
Josh Beckett
Cheryl Ford
Tony Gonzalez
Ellen MacArthur
Tracy McGrady
Steve McNair
Ryan Newman
Tanya Streeter
Natasha Watley

World Leaders

VOLUME 1: Environmental Leaders 1

Edward Abbey
Renee Askins
David Brower
Rachel Carson
Marjory Stoneman Douglas
Dave Foreman
Lois Gibbs
Wangari Maathai
Chico Mendes
Russell A. Mittermeier
Margaret and Olaus J. Murie
Patsy Ruth Oliver
Roger Tory Peterson
Ken Saro-Wiwa
Paul Watson
Adam Werbach

VOLUME 2: Modern African Leaders

Mohammed Farah Aidid
Idi Amin
Hastings Kamuzu Banda
Haile Selassie
Hassan II
Kenneth Kaunda
Jomo Kenyatta
Winnie Mandela
Mobutu Sese Seko
Robert Mugabe
Kwame Nkrumah
Julius Kambarage Nyerere
Anwar Sadat
Jonas Savimbi
Léopold Sédar Senghor
William V. S. Tubman

VOLUME 3: Environmental Leaders 2

John Cronin
Dai Qing
Ka Hsaw Wa
Winona LaDuke
Aldo Leopold
Bernard Martin
Cynthia Moss
John Muir
Gaylord Nelson
Douglas Tompkins
Hazel Wolf